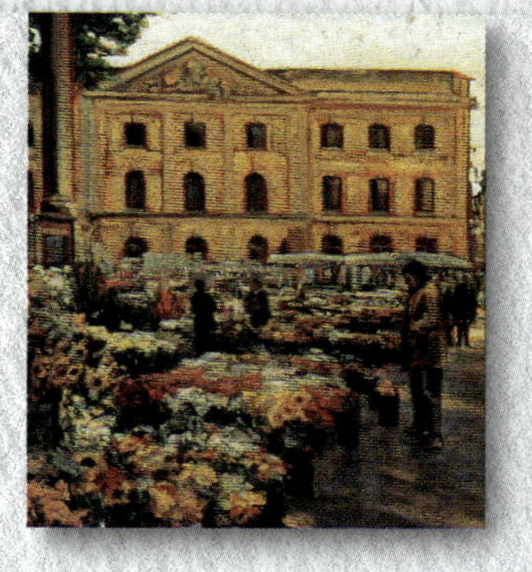

Street Scenes

Around the World

Street scenes make spectacular painting subjects because they offer such a diverse range of locations—from a simple Tuscan doorway to a complex Manhattan street where taxis jockey for position. This book explores the painting methods used by four accomplished oil painters, each with a unique approach regarding subjects, tools, and techniques. Individually they'll guide you step by step through painting a French flower market, a canyon drive, a chef's afternoon break, a German sidewalk cafe, and more. And, along the way, you'll learn the basics of oil painting and pick up special tips and insights from each artist. With every engaging lesson, you'll discover the information and inspiration you need to select your own subjects, mix your own colors, develop your own style, and paint your own breathtaking street scenes in oil!

CONTENTS

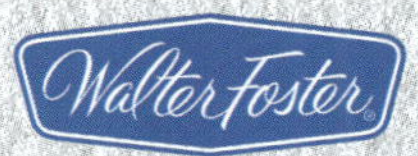

Gathering the Essentials

A trip to any art supply store will quickly help you realize the vast number of tools, equipment, and products available to painters. It's easy to get excited and want to bring home one of everything; but the good news is that you need only a few materials to get started. A good guideline is to think of your shopping as an investment—buy the best products you can afford; if you take good care of your brushes, paints, and palette, they can last a long time, and your paintings will last for generations. The basic items you'll need are described here, but for more information, refer to *Oil Painting Materials and Their Uses* by William F. Powell in Walter Foster's Artist's Library series.

BUYING OIL PAINTS

In the store, you may notice a price discrepancy between different grades of paint called "students' grade" and "artists' grade." Even though artists' grade paints will require a bit more of an expense upfront, these paints contain better-quality pigment and fewer additives, which translates into colors that are more intense and will stay true longer—making them worth the extra money.

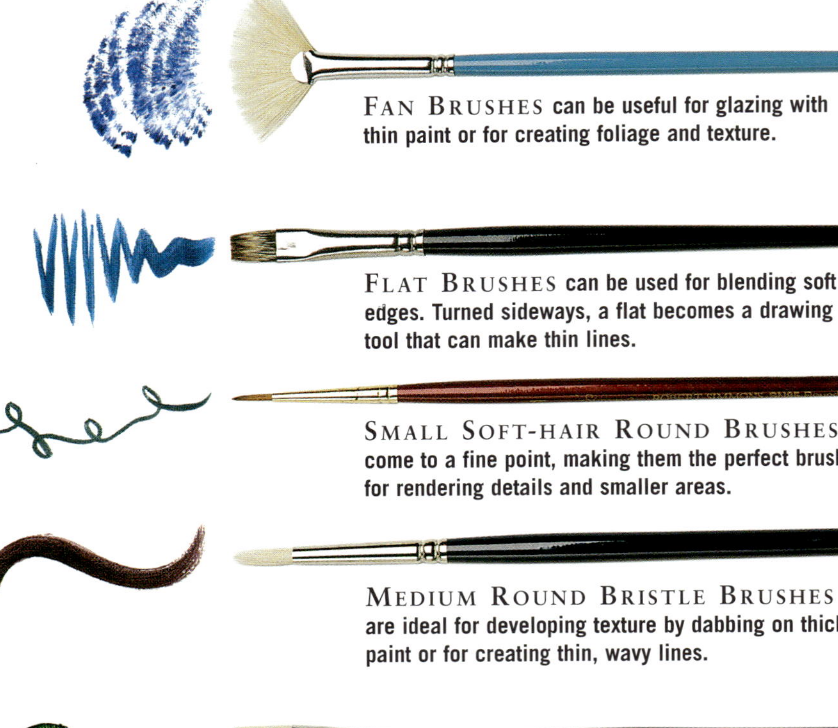

FLAT BRUSHES can be used for blending soft edges. Turned sideways, a flat becomes a drawing tool that can make thin lines.

SMALL SOFT-HAIR ROUND BRUSHES come to a fine point, making them the perfect brush for rendering details and smaller areas.

MEDIUM ROUND BRISTLE BRUSHES are ideal for developing texture by dabbing on thick paint or for creating thin, wavy lines.

MEDIUM BRIGHT BRUSHES are flat with shorter bristles and are ideal for scrubbing in foliage or creating texture.

BRISTLE-HAIR FILBERTS are efficient brushes for blocking in and painting large areas, as they can hold a substantial amount of paint.

CHOOSING A PALETTE OF COLORS

A good basic palette will include the nine colors shown below, which includes a warm and cool version of each of the primary colors. (See page 4.) The artists featured in this book also use some unique colors in their palettes, listed with each project, which will give you an opportunity to experiment with different options. Keep in mind that there is always more than one way to mix a color; once you understand the basics of color theory, you can get a better feel for the art of mixing color. (For more on color, please see pages 4–5.)

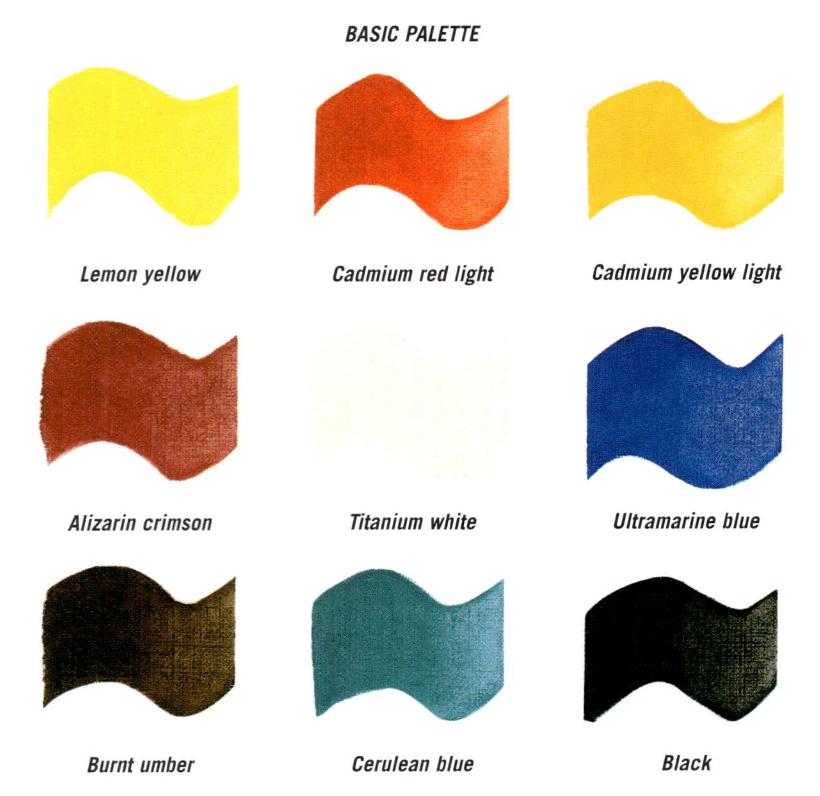

BASIC PALETTE

Lemon yellow	*Cadmium red light*	*Cadmium yellow light*
Alizarin crimson	*Titanium white*	*Ultramarine blue*
Burnt umber	*Cerulean blue*	*Black*

BUYING AND CARING FOR BRUSHES

Oil painting brushes come in a variety of sizes, shapes, and textures. Some brushes are sized by number, and others are sized by inches. A universal standard for brush sizes does not exist, so sizes will vary slightly among suppliers. Buy brushes that are appropriate for the size of the work you will be creating. Also note how the brush feels in your hand: Your comfort level will relate directly to the amount of time you will want to be in front of your easel. Brushes can also be categorized by the material of their bristles: natural-hair or synthetic. Most artists use a combination of both types. Cleaning and caring for your brushes is essential—always rinse them well with turpentine and store them bristle side up or flat (never bristle side down).

SELECTING SUPPORTS

The *support* is the surface on which you paint. Although oil artists paint on many surfaces, wood and canvas are the most common. You can stretch your own canvas, but it's easier to buy preprimed and prestretched canvas (stapled to a frame) or canvas glued to cardboard. If you choose a porous material, such as wood, first apply primer to seal the surface so your paints will adhere to the support (instead of being absorbed by it).

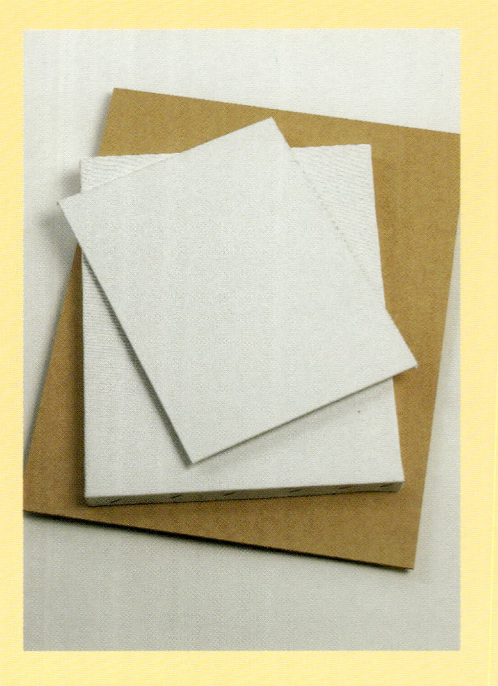

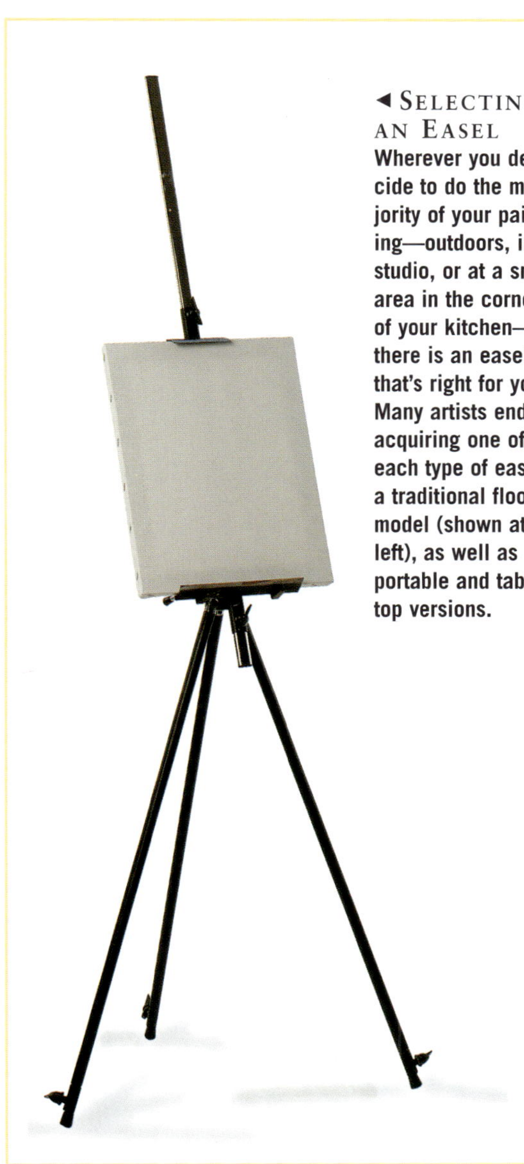

◄ **SELECTING AN EASEL**
Wherever you decide to do the majority of your painting—outdoors, in a studio, or at a small area in the corner of your kitchen—there is an easel that's right for you. Many artists end up acquiring one of each type of easel: a traditional floor model (shown at left), as well as portable and table-top versions.

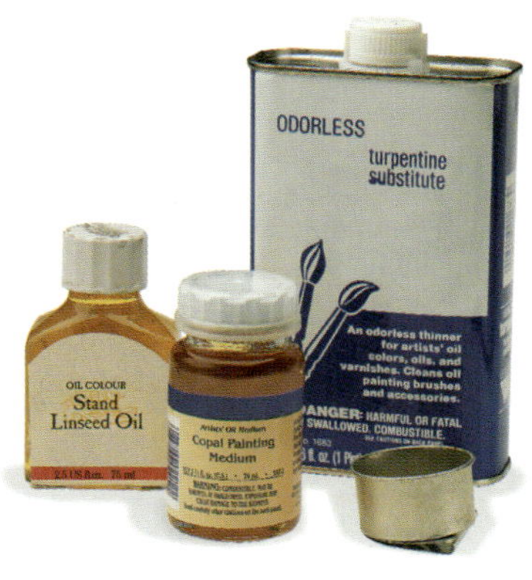

▲ **ADDING MEDIUMS**
In addition to the medium you buy, be sure to purchase a glass or metal container to hold the medium. Some paint cups have built-in clips that attach easily to your mixing palette.

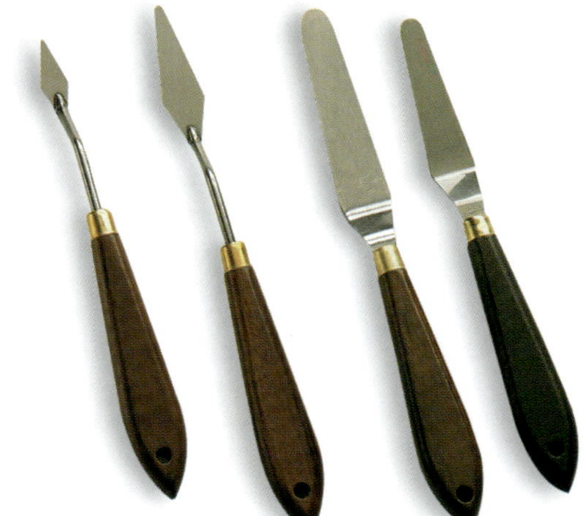

▼ **COLLECTING EXTRAS**
Basic tools are all necessities, but you may also want to acquire a silk sea sponge and an old toothbrush to render special effects. Even though you may not use these additional items for every oil painting you work on, it's a good idea to keep them on hand in case you need them. And when you have spare moments, you can experiment with creating different effects.

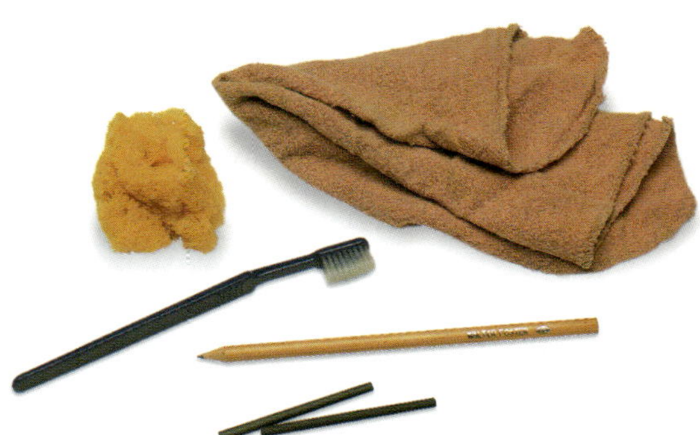

◄ **USING PAINTING AND PALETTE KNIVES**
Palette knives can be used either as tools to apply paint to your support or to mix paint on your palette. Look for knives with raised handles, which help you avoid getting wet paint on your hand as you work. A palette (mixing) knife has a longer, more rectangular head, whereas a painting knife usually has a smaller, diamond-shaped head.

UTILIZING ADDITIVES

You can modify the consistency of your paint with mediums and thinners. Additives include *linseed oil*, which thins out the paint, and *copal*, which speeds drying time; others can alter the finish or texture of the paint. You will also need to buy some type of oil medium, since you will need to moisten the paint when it dries. Mediums also let you create glazes with layers of thin paint. Turpentine or mineral spirits can be used to clean your brushes and to thin the paint for initial washes or underpaintings, but you won't want to use them as mediums. They break down the paint, whereas the oil mediums you add actually help preserve the paint.

PICKING A PALETTE

The mixing palette you choose—plastic, wood, glass, or paper—must be easy to clean and big enough for mixing colors. Glass is very durable and a great surface for mixing paints. Disposable palette paper makes for simple cleanup, and if you choose this option, you can always buy an airtight plastic box to keep your excess paint fresh till your next painting session. Store-bought palettes generally have a hole for the thumb at one end, making them comfortable to hold. Experiment with different materials and tools and pay attention to your personal comfort: It will make your painting time more enjoyable.

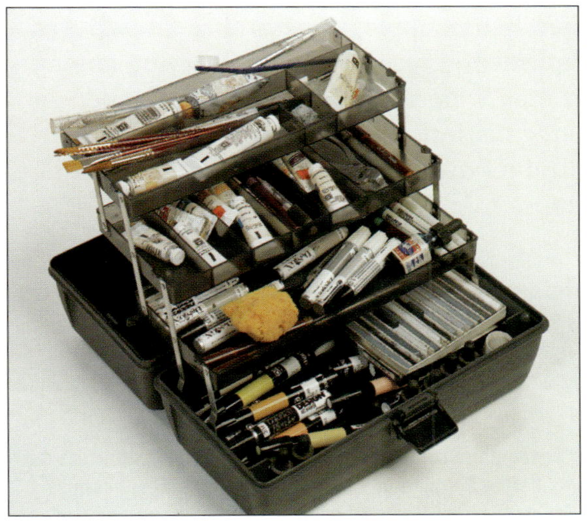

GETTING ORGANIZED Paint boxes are great for organizing your supplies—you can work straight from the box without packing and unpacking! And these boxes also make storing and transporting your tools and materials convenient.

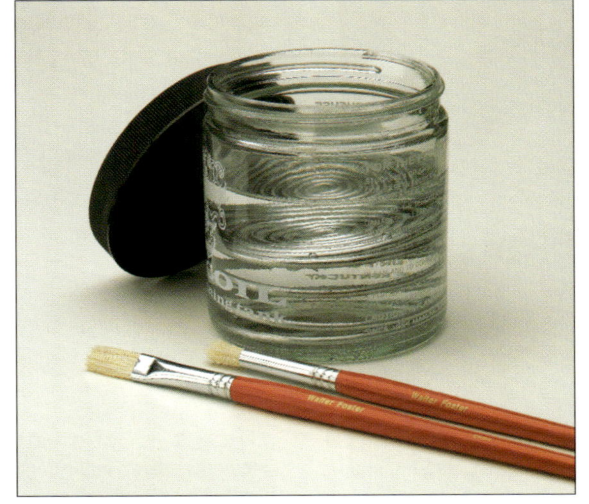

CLEANING BRUSHES Buying a jar with a screen or coil in the bottom saves on cleanup time. Rubbing the brush against the coil loosens paint. Use soap and warm (not hot) water to remove residual paint. Lay out your brushes to dry.

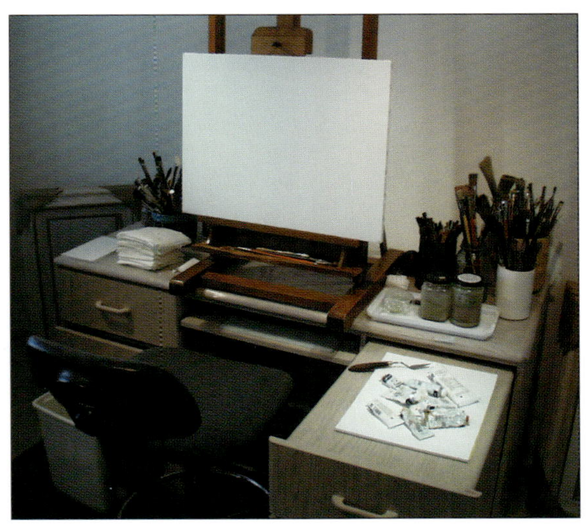

SETTING UP A WORK STATION Keep all your supplies in the same place so each time you are ready to paint, you don't waste time searching for anything. Natural light or sufficient artificial lighting is a must, as is comfort!

COLOR THEORY

A color wheel is a helpful tool

for understanding color. The three *primary* colors (yellow, red, and blue) are the basis for the other colors on the wheel. The *secondary* colors (orange, green and purple) are all combinations of two primaries, and *tertiary* colors (such as red-purple or yellow-green) are mixes of a primary and a secondary. Colors directly across from each other on the wheel are *complementary*, whereas groups of adjacent colors are *analogous*. The word *hue* refers to the color itself, such as red or yellow-green; *intensity* refers to the color's strength; and *value* means the relative lightness or darkness of a color or of black.

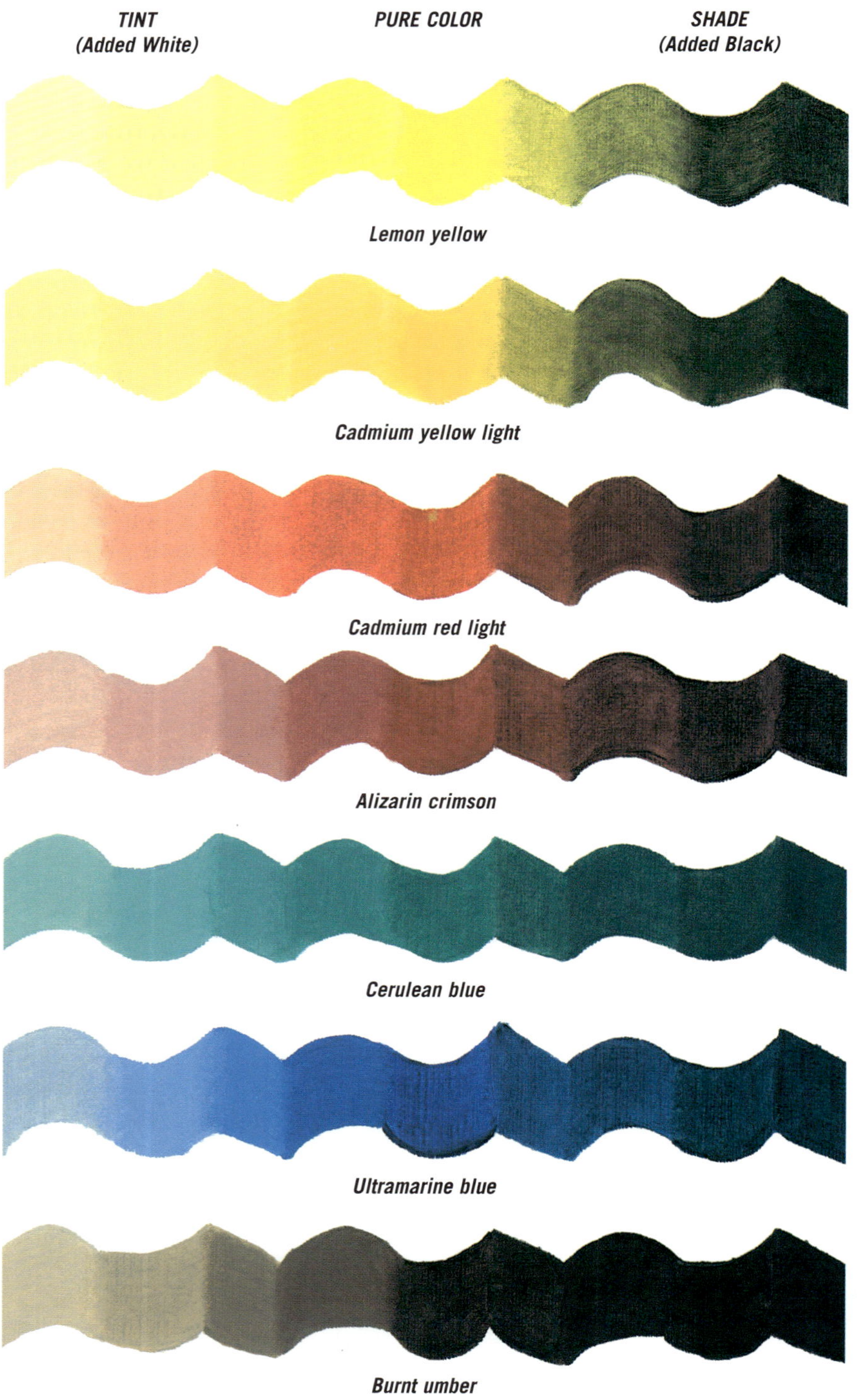

TINTS AND SHADES The chart above shows varying tints and shades of different colors. The pure color is in the middle of each example; the tints are to the left, and the shades are to the right.

The ability to create feeling—as well as interest and unity—in your artwork comes from knowing the fundamentals of how colors relate to each other and interact. You can mix just about every color from the three primaries. But all primaries are not created alike, so you'll eventually want to have at least two versions of each primary, one warm and one cool. (See page 5.) These two primary sets will give you a wide range of secondary mixes.

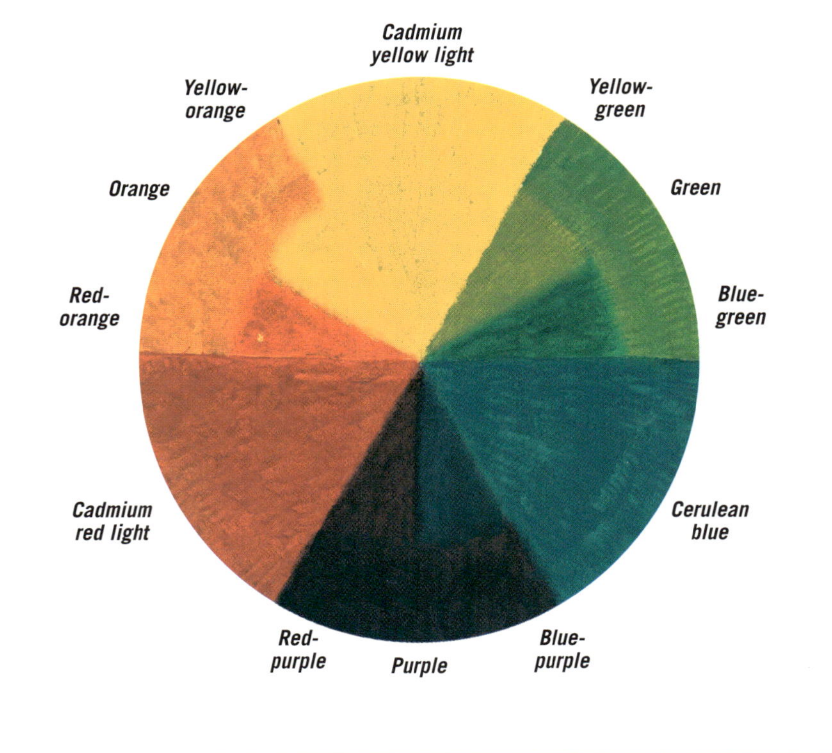

VALUE

The illusion of depth and form throughout a painting is created by the placement of varying values on your canvas. On the color wheel, yellow has the lightest value and purple has the darkest value. You can change the value of any color by adding white or black. (See the chart at left.) Adding white to a pure color results in a lighter value *tint* of that color, adding black results in a darker value *shade*, and adding gray results in a *tone*. (A *monochromatic* painting is created with tints, shades, and tones of only one color.) In a painting, the very lightest values are referred to as the *highlights* and the very darkest values are the *shadows*.

COMPLEMENTARY COLORS

As noted above, complements are any two colors directly opposite each other on the color wheel, such as green and red, orange and blue, or yellow and purple. When placed next to each other, complementary colors create visual interest, but when mixed, they neutralize (or "gray") one another. For example, to neutralize a bright red, mix in a touch of its complement: green. By mixing varying amounts of each color, you can create a wide range of neutral grays and browns. (In painting, mixing neutrals is preferable to using them straight from a tube; neutral mixtures provide richer, more realistic colors that are closer to those found in nature.)

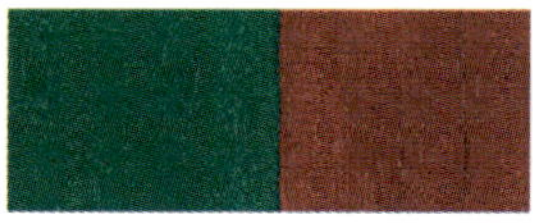 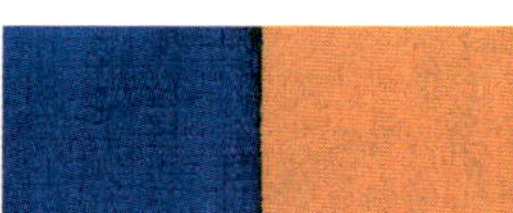 

DIRECT COMPLEMENTS These pairs of color swatches are examples of direct complements. Using color complements can add drama or vitality to your paintings, because direct complements create the most striking contrasts when placed next to one another.

UNDERSTANDING COLOR PSYCHOLOGY

The red, orange, and yellow colors on one side of the color wheel are considered to be "warm," while the blues, greens, and purples on the other half of the wheel are thought of as "cool" colors. Warm colors can convey energy and excitement, whereas cool colors usually evoke a calm, peaceful mood. Within all families of colors, there are both warm and cool hues. A cool red (such as alizarin crimson) contains more blue, and a warm red (such as cadmium red) contains more yellow. Keep in mind that cool colors tend to recede, while warmer colors appear to "pop" forward. Knowing the properties and effects of various colors is especially relevant for painting street scenes, as you can use color to help portray a sense of distance.

MIXING COLORS

Mixing colors efficiently and successfully is a learned skill: The more you practice, the better you will become. In order to accurately copy what you are seeing in your subject, the most important thing to do is train your eye to really see the shapes of color in an object—the varying hues, values, tints, tones, and shades. Once you can see them, you can practice mixing them. Whether you're a beginner or a painter that has logged many studio hours, you may want to step outside and practice mixing some of the colors you see in nature at different times of day. Notice how colors seem to change as the light changes; the ability to discern the variations in color under different lighting conditions is one of the keys to successful color mixing.

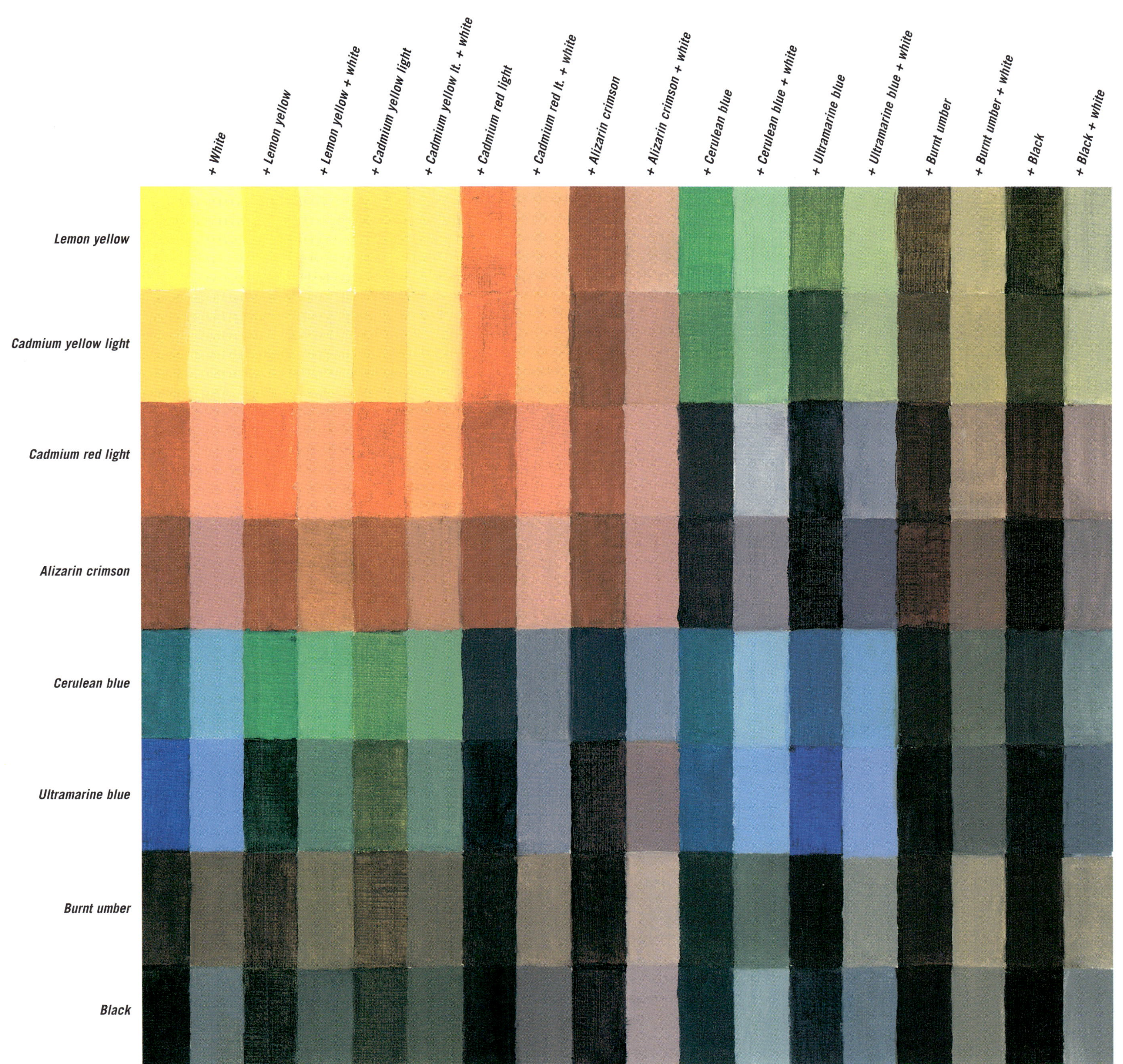

USING A LIMITED PALETTE You don't need to purchase dozens of tubes of paint to be able to mix a vast array of hues. Instead you can use a limited number of paints and mix the other colors you need. The chart above shows just some of the colors that can be made using the nine colors found in the basic palette listed on page 2. You may want to create your own chart using the colors from your palette; this is an excellent exercise for learning to mix color.

PAINTING FROM PHOTOS

WITH TOM SWIMM

Many artists prefer to paint subjects from life, but there are times when painting on location can be impractical, or even impossible! When you're inspired by fleeting images—such as the ever-changing light, color, and energy found on a busy city street—capturing the scene on canvas can present a challenge. One way artists meet this challenge is by using photo references. In essence, recording a moment on film stops the clock, giving you, the artist, the luxury of time. With a photo reference, you can study the scene before beginning your painting, making it much easier to replicate the excitement you witnessed in person or to experiment with changes in the composition of the active scene. Tom Swimm's painting of a rain-slicked Manhattan street is a near-replica of a photo he took. But because it was difficult to control the composition with the constant state of flux and distraction, Tom didn't wait for an ideal moment of inspiration to point and click. Instead he photographed the scene from various points of view, making his final choice once he returned to his studio.

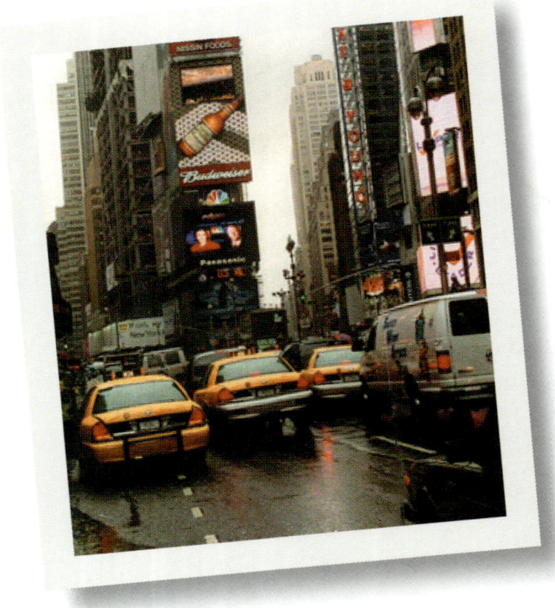

CROPPING IN After reviewing a number of photos I took of this busy city scene, I selected this one for my painting. Once I had the time to study the composition, I decided there were too many visual distractions. I changed the composition to establish a clear focus by cropping in on the scene to create a more intimate feel than my original photo offered.

alizarin crimson, brilliant yellow, cadmium red, cadmium red light, cadmium orange light, cadmium yellow light, cerulean blue, flesh, light blue violet, Payne's gray, phthalo violet, Prussian blue, raw sienna, titanium white, yellow ochre

DARK VALUES

Prussian blue + alizarin crimson

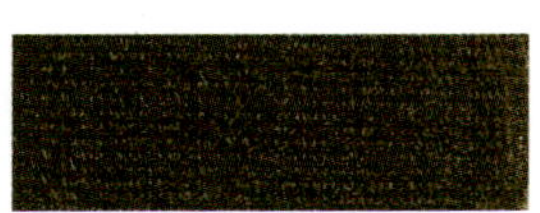

Prussian blue + alizarin crimson + Payne's gray + cadmium red

Prussian blue + alizarin crimson + yellow ochre

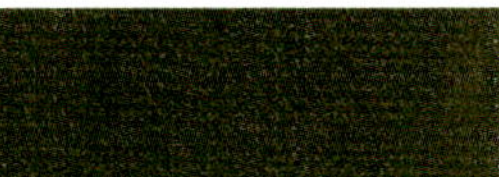

Prussian blue + alizarin crimson + raw sienna

1 Magenta gives me a nice warm undertone for my yellow taxis, so I start by covering the canvas with a base coat of acrylic magenta. (Choosing a cooler color as an undertone, such as cerulean blue, might give a greenish tinge to my yellow taxis, which is something I want to avoid.) Many artists prefer to use oil for their base coat, but I use acrylic for one simple reason: It dries faster. And after selecting my subject and sketching my composition, I'm eager to start as quickly as possible. I'm now ready to begin with the oils.

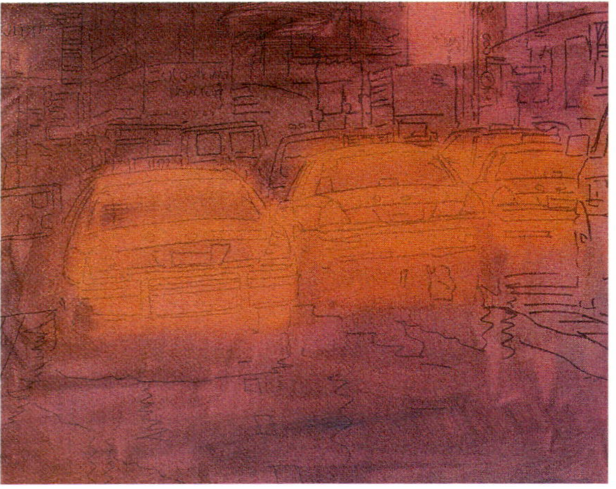

2 I begin my underpainting with a very loose and simple wash of only four colors: yellow ochre, burnt sienna, cerulean blue, and Payne's gray. I want the paint to be very thin and transparent at this stage, so I thin it with oil painting medium. I also use a large flat brush, as I'm not concerned with detail yet. I start by blocking in yellow ochre for the taxis; then I block in the background buildings using burnt sienna mixed with Payne's gray. For the foreground buildings, I add a little cerulean blue to the mix.

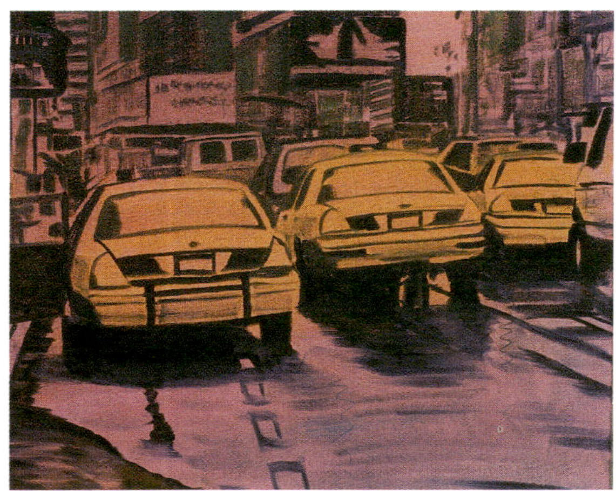

3 I am ready to define the darkest areas of my painting, so I set up my palette with a mixture of the darkest values. I never use black; instead I use very dark blues, reds, and greens I've mixed myself. (See "Dark Values" above.) Here I've combined Prussian blue and alizarin crimson to create a very deep violet for the building outlines and the details on the taxis and in the shadow areas beneath the cabs. I also add raw sienna or yellow ochre to this mixture to create the basic shapes that will guide the next steps.

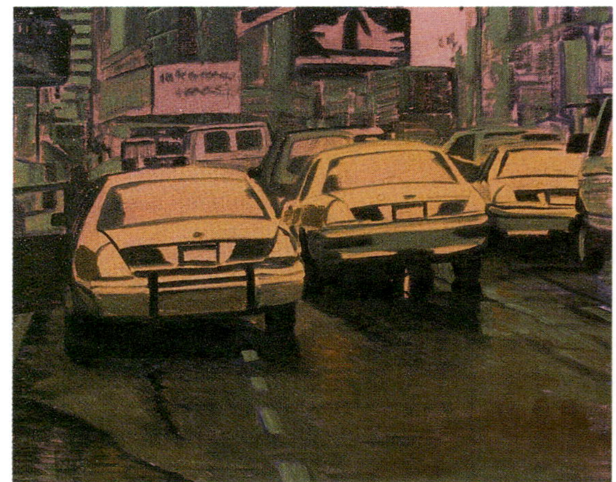

4 Next I add Payne's gray and cadmium red light to the Prussian blue and alizarin crimson mix. I place this color in some of the darker areas to vary the color temperature. Then, using the same colors from step three, I begin developing detail, using cerulean blue for the buildings and the shadow areas beneath the taxis. I also add the first layer of color to the pavement with this mixture, adding burnt sienna on top of that to vary the color and texture in the reflections. My dark values are still distinct here.

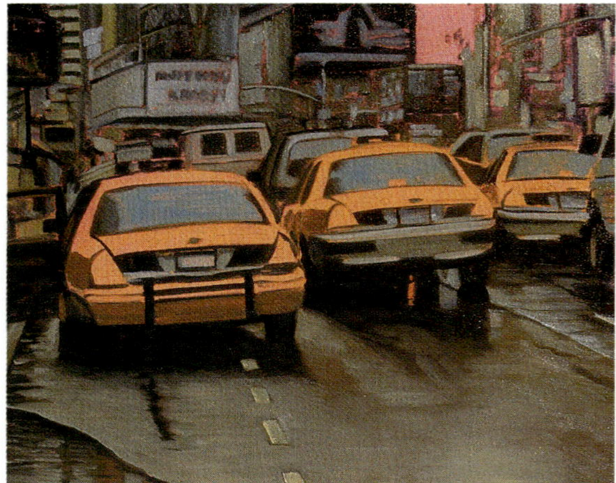

5 To define the middle values, I first create new color mixtures. (See "Middle Values" on page 7.) Now I begin adding random shapes to buildings, filling in some of the negative areas. Using a large flat brush and varying my brushstrokes, I work on all areas of the painting, being careful not to overwork any one spot. This method helps me harmonize and tie in visual elements. Next I load the brush with thicker paint and apply broad strokes to the street. Then I add detail to the taxis on the windows and bumpers.

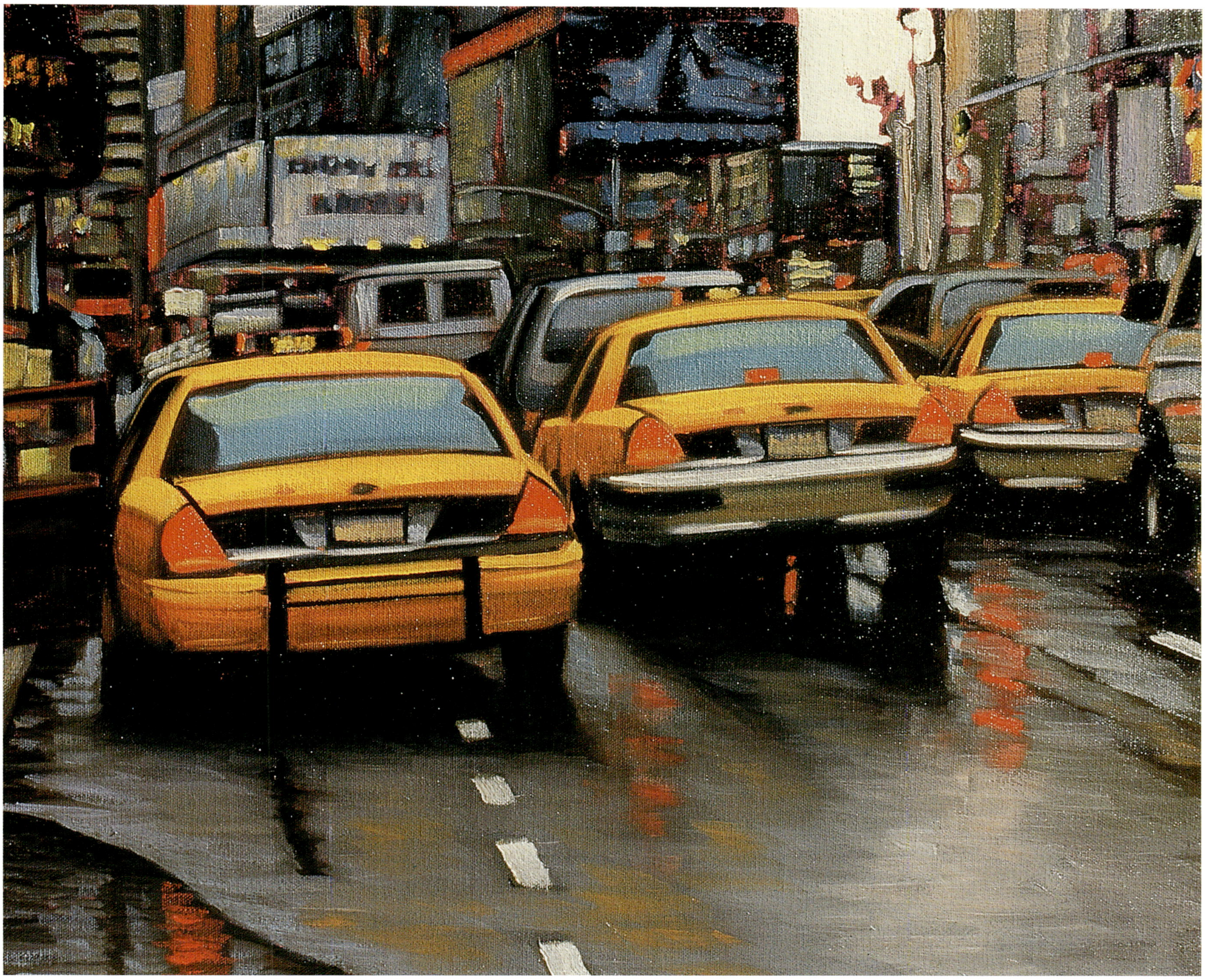

7 As you can see, in each step, I've added just enough detail to create the impression of the elements; yet at this stage, the painting has developed into a very realistic scene. Now it's time for the final highlights. Using the yellow and orange mix, I paint the brightest areas of the taxis, blending this color into the shadow areas while the paint is still wet. I add the same color to some of the buildings and the street reflections for balance. I also apply a mixture of cadmium red and phthalo violet to the tail-lights, the street reflections, and some of the buildings. At this point in the painting, I step back and let my eye wander around the composition; then I make any minor adjustments needed. I also compare the painting to my original photograph to see if I captured the same impact of energy and urban intimacy. When I'm happy with the result, I put down my brush and proclaim the painting complete.

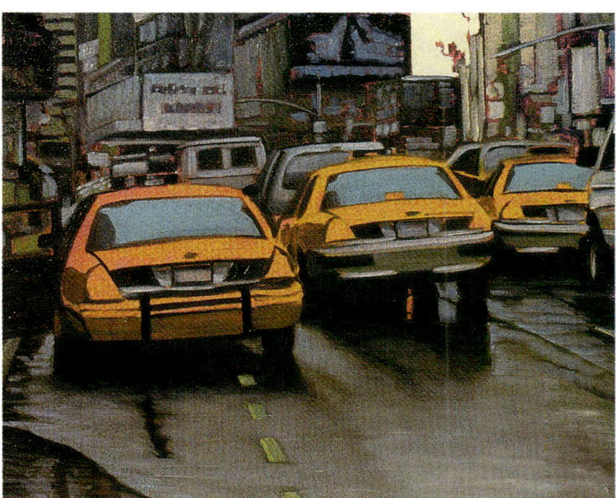

6 Now I mix new colors for my highlights (see "Light Values" at right), switching to a small flat brush for the fine details. I paint the sky area first, mixing a bit of cerulean blue with a lot of white. This color block enhances the overall brightness of my values, giving me a full range of values in my final painting. Next I lighten the background buildings with the cerulean blue and yellow ochre mix; then I brighten the taxi windows and bumpers. I finish this stage by applying a layer of light blue violet on the pavement.

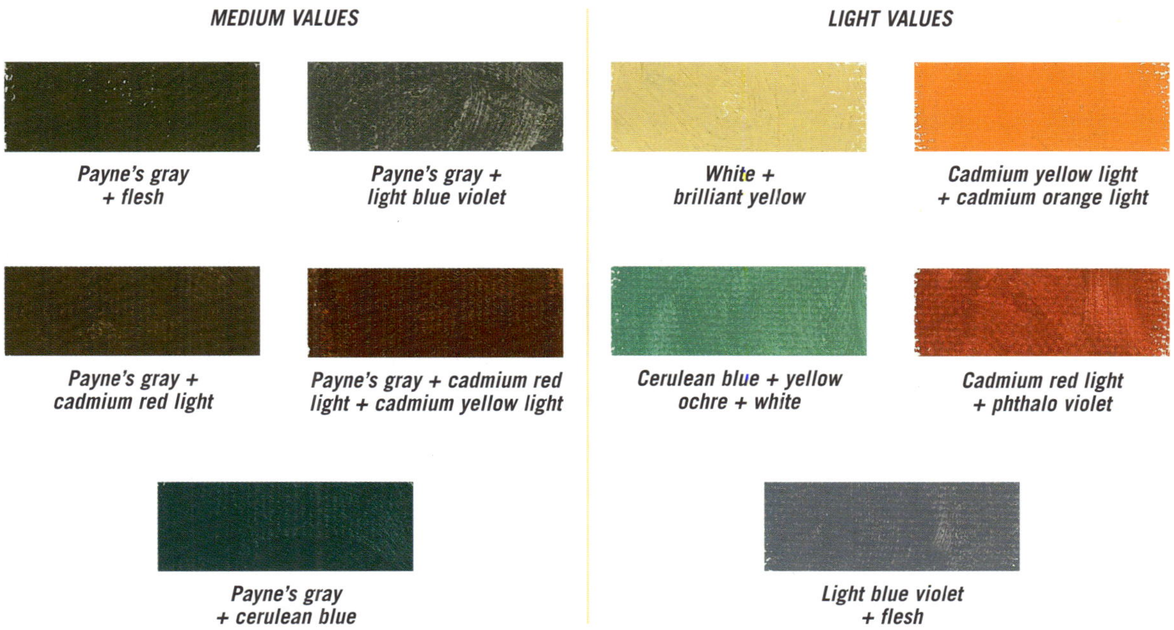

MEDIUM VALUES

Payne's gray + flesh

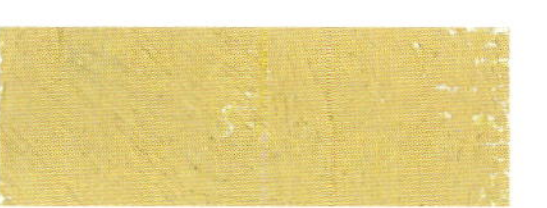
Payne's gray + light blue violet

Payne's gray + cadmium red light

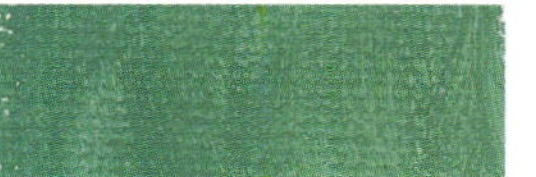
Payne's gray + cadmium red light + cadmium yellow light

Payne's gray + cerulean blue

LIGHT VALUES

White + brilliant yellow

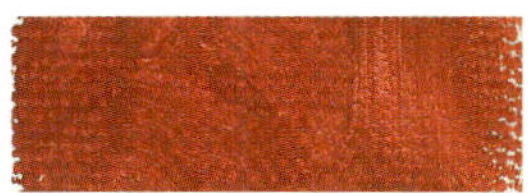
Cadmium yellow light + cadmium orange light

Cerulean blue + yellow ochre + white

Cadmium red light + phthalo violet

Light blue violet + flesh

Balancing with Neutrals

with Tom Swimm

Primary colors make a strong statement in a painting, brightening the canvas and drawing attention. But a painting created with bold primary colors alone can distract and overwhelm the viewer. Including more subdued neutrals—such as beiges, browns, and grays—provides a balance to the visually exciting primary colors. In this German café scene painted by Tom Swimm, the neutral tones offer a resting point for the eyes, so the viewer can take in the eye-catching reds, yellows, and blues of the focal point without experiencing sensory overload.

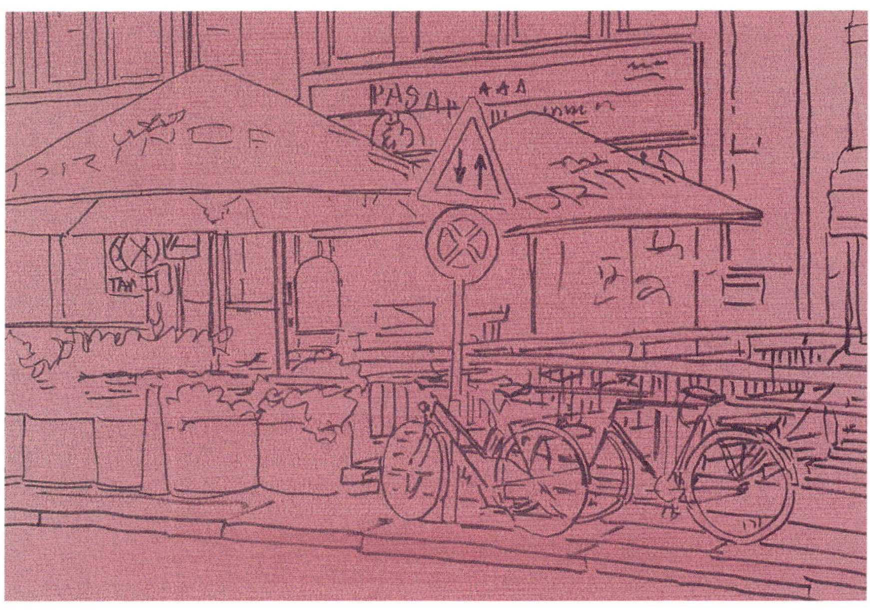

1 To begin, I make a loose drawing of the basic shapes directly onto the canvas, placing the bicycles in the foreground to direct the viewer's eye into the scene and toward the umbrellas, which are the dominant motif. Next I cover the canvas with an acrylic base of medium magenta. Notice that this layer is transparent so my drawing is still visible; these faint guidelines will provide a solid visual foundation for the composition of my painting.

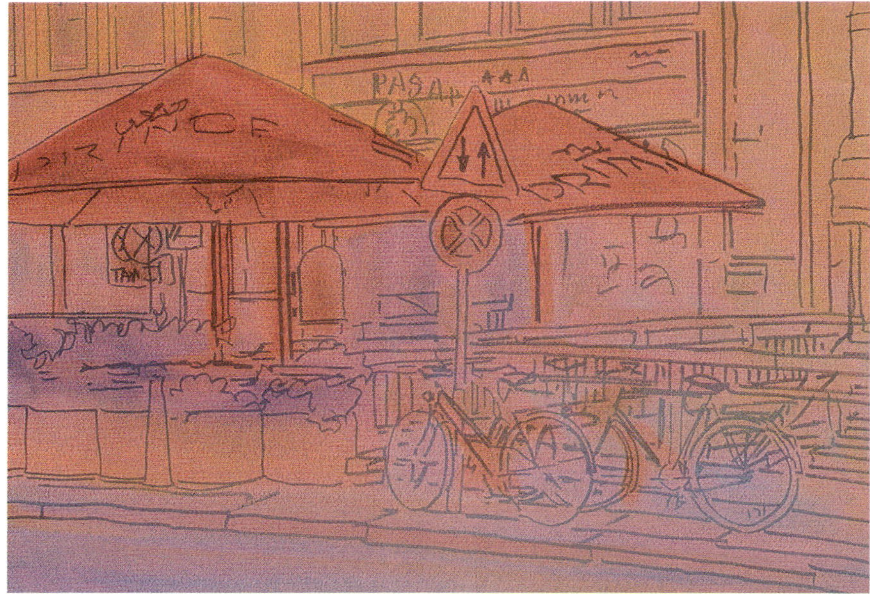

2 Once the base coat is thoroughly dry, I begin defining the basic shapes and tonal values. At this stage, I use only four colors on the palette: yellow ochre for the building facades, violet gray for the street, and burnt sienna for the umbrellas; I add Payne's gray for the areas in shadow. After thinning the colors with oil painting medium, I apply the underpainting with a large flat sable brush, keeping the brushstrokes loose.

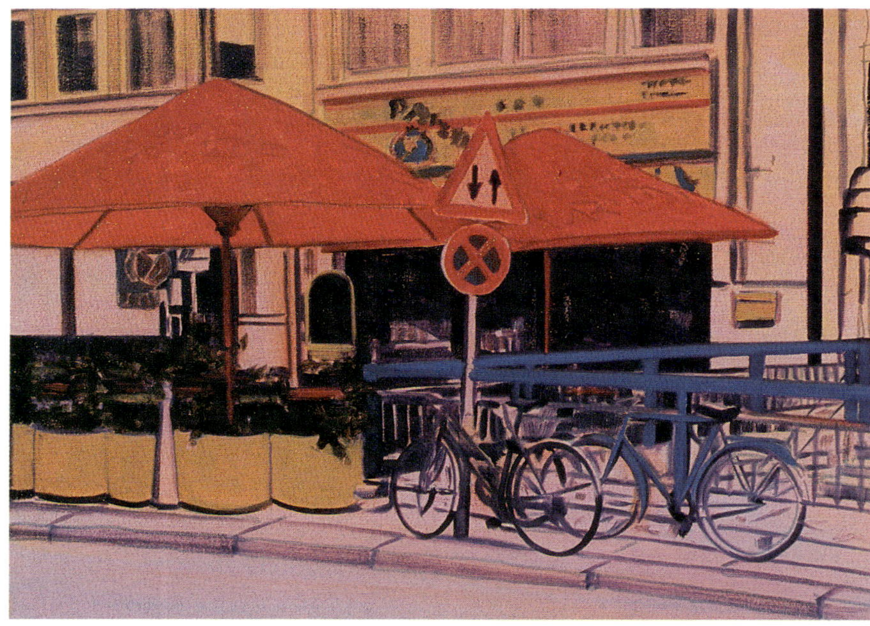

3 Now, to begin establishing depth and defining the shapes, I apply the darks (shown below). With a large, flat sable brush, I paint the windows and the dark shadow areas using a mix of Payne's gray and dioxazine purple. I also use this color to outline the sidewalk and the smaller railings. Next I use cerulean blue mixed with dioxazine purple to add shape to the railings and the bicycle on the right. I apply alizarin crimson mixed with cadmium red for the umbrellas and some sign details. Then I create flower pots and other sign elements with raw sienna. I accent the foliage with a sap green and yellow ochre mix.

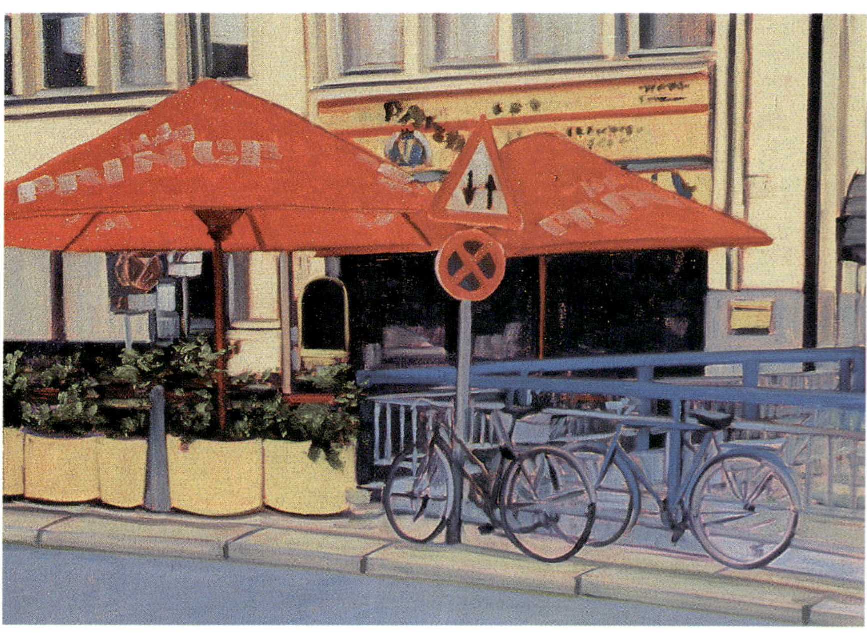

4 Having established my darks, I move to the mid-range tones, painting the larger areas of color. Here I use thicker paint to solidify the forms, fully loading the brush. I also alter the brushstroke direction for a more "painterly" effect. I mix medium-value colors of similar intensities to create a sense of balance and harmony in my painting. (Experiment when mixing colors to see how intensity can vary, primarily as you add more or less white.) For the building, I use raw sienna; the sidewalk and pavement are cerulean blue. At this point, I begin adding details to the bicycles, railings, windows, and signs.

DARK VALUES

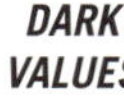 

Payne's gray + dioxazine purple

Cerulean blue + dioxazine purple

Sap green + yellow ochre

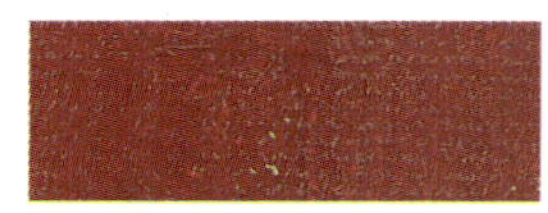

Alizarin crimson + cadmium red

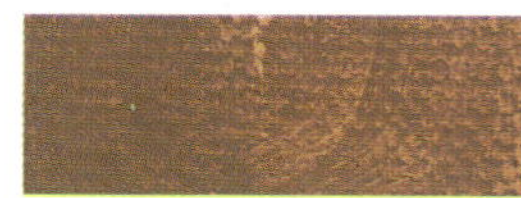

Raw sienna

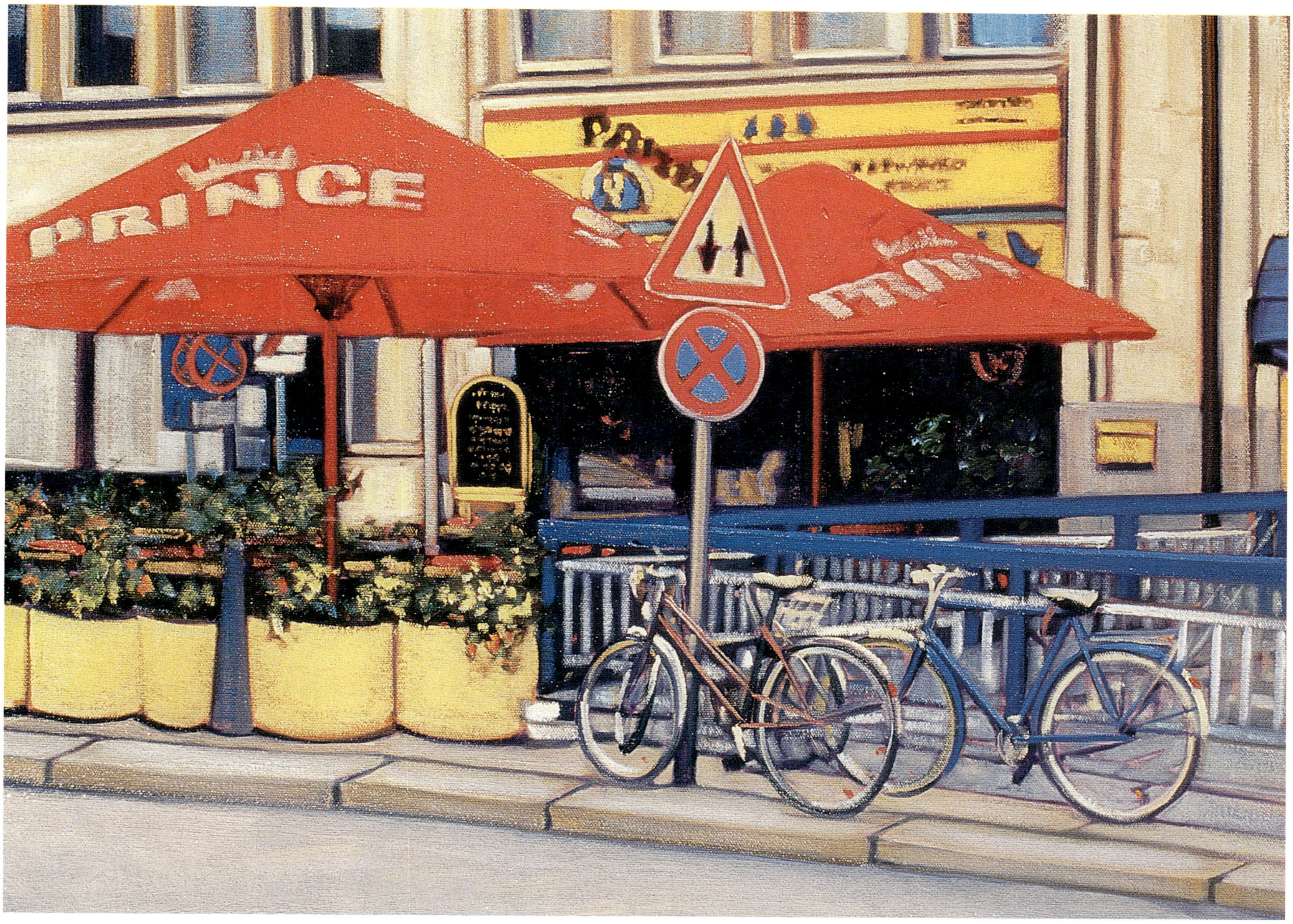

7 Now it's time for the finishing touches! I mix lighter colors on my palette by adding white to brilliant yellow, flesh, and cadmium orange light. I highlight areas of the foreground with this mixture, and then apply highlights to the bicycles, including the seats and tires. I finish the lettering on the umbrellas too. As I paint, I stay loose and spontaneous, stepping back to check my progress. At this stage, I trust my instincts and don't overwork the details. When I'm happy with the results, I'm finished with the painting.

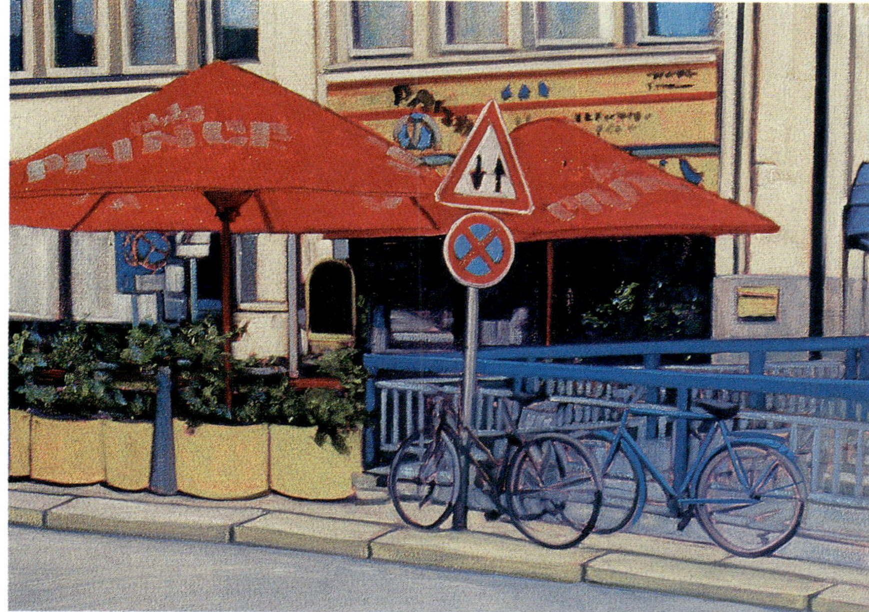

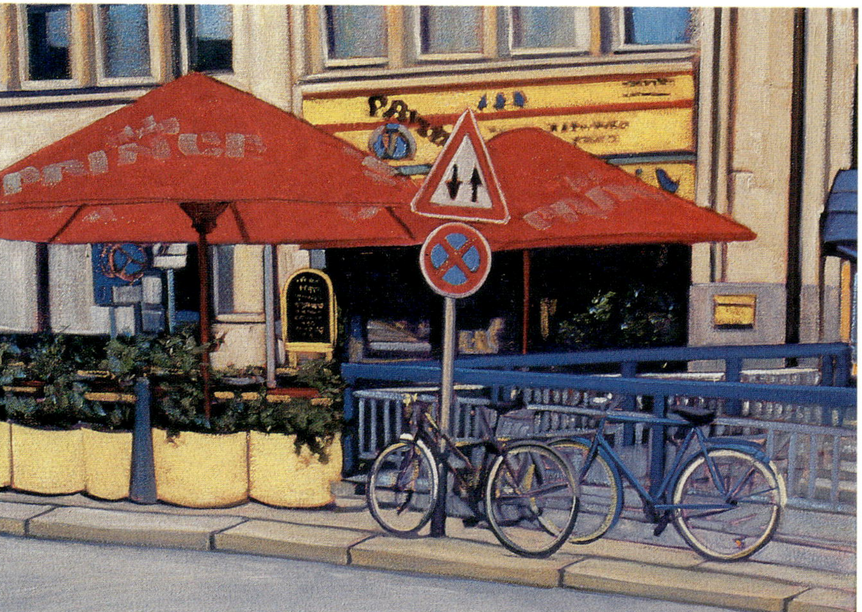

5 Next I add a little white to the medium values from step four before continuing to layer. I heighten the contrast in the building façade, sidewalk, and pavement. Then I do the same to the details, such as the signs, posts, and railings. I let the underpainting guide me, allowing some of it to peek through for depth and visual interest. There are a lot of subtle blues in the scene, so I mix some variations of phthalo blue, cerulean blue, and Prussian blue (see below) and apply these blues with the edge of a flat sable brush. Using my brush as a drawing tool, I render some of the unfinished areas, such as the sign details, windows, and awnings.

6 My goal with this painting is to develop a strong harmony of primary colors that form a nice balance in the composition. To enhance this unity of colors, I finish layering the yellows and reds, applying the paint thickly. I use cadmium red light for the umbrellas and some smaller accents. A mix of cadmium yellow light with cadmium orange light brightens the large sign on the building. After I add more white to this mixture, I use it to model the flower pots in the foreground and highlight areas on the bicycles. Notice that even a small highlight can produce a greater sense of definition.

BLUE MIXES

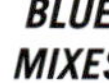 

Phthalo blue + white

Phthalo blue + white + sap green

Prussian blue + white

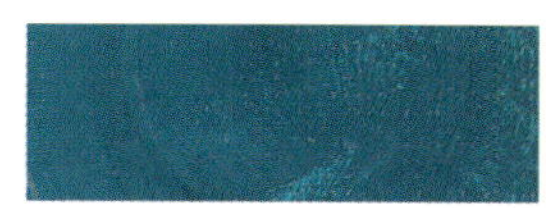

Cerulean blue + white

Cerulean blue + white + flesh

Developing a Strong Composition

with Tom Swimm

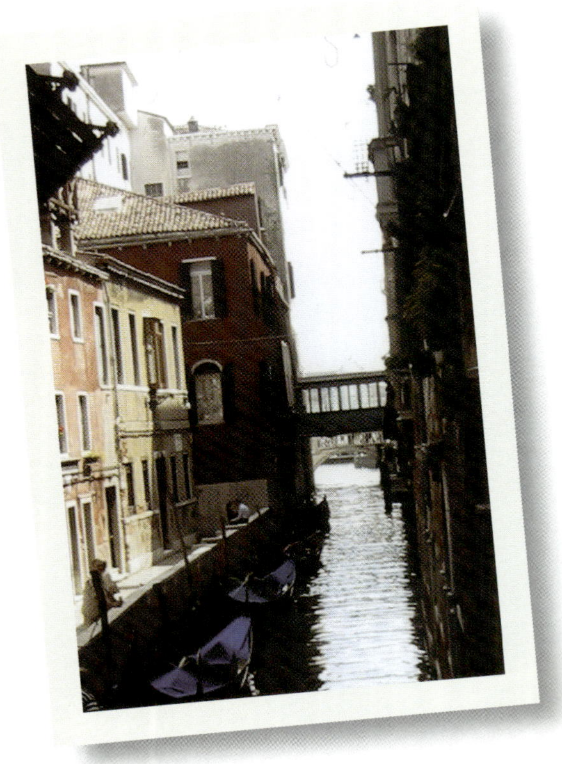

Taking Artistic License Although you can't plan the arrangement of objects in a street scene, you can alter the composition and even change the colors to suit yourself.

Composition is an important element of any painting. Ideally a good composition directs the viewer's eye in and around the painting through the use of interesting shapes, colors, and lines. And an effective visual path always leads to the center of interest, or *focal point.* In a strong composition, the focal point is typically placed off-center to create more dynamism. In addition, good compositions usually contain overlapping objects that provide a sense of depth. Tom Swimm incorporates all the rules of good composition as he paints an inspiring street that isn't really a street at all. By cropping in tightly, Tom deliberately heightens interest in the scene, exaggerating the sense of perspective. At the same time, the viewpoint shifts the canal away from the center of the composition, resulting in a more natural balance. Finally Tom eliminates extraneous visual clutter from the composition to create a clear visual path to the focal point, the water-paved Venetian canal.

Color Palette

alizarin crimson, brilliant yellow, burnt sienna, cadmium orange, cadmium red, cadmium red light, cadmium yellow light, cerulean blue, flesh, light blue violet, Payne's gray, phthalo violet, Prussian blue, raw sienna, sap green, titanium white, yellow ochre

DARK VALUES

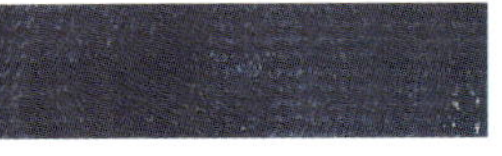

Prussian blue + cerulean blue + phthalo violet

Payne's gray + raw sienna

Payne's gray + flesh + yellow ochre

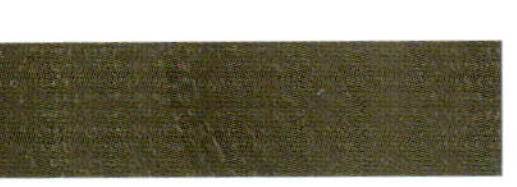

Payne's gray + yellow ochre

Payne's gray + yellow ochre + phthalo violet

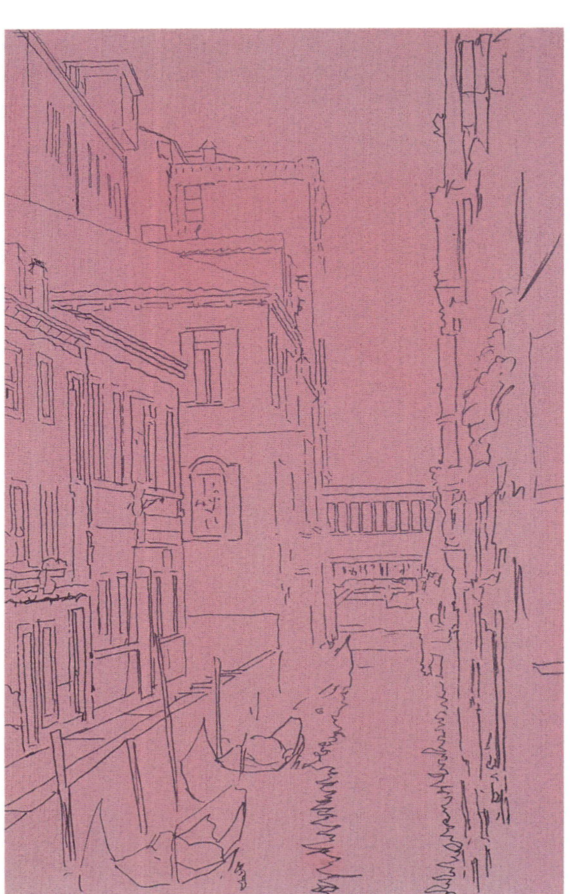

1 After I sketch the main shapes of my composition, I cover the entire canvas with a thin coat of magenta acrylic paint. When the acrylic dries, I establish the fundamental values by applying an underpainting of thick color blocks. At this stage, I rely on just five colors: flesh and light blue violet for the sky and water; and burnt sienna, raw sienna, and Payne's gray for the buildings and gondolas. Using a very large flat brush, I apply the thinned oil colors with loose, broad strokes.

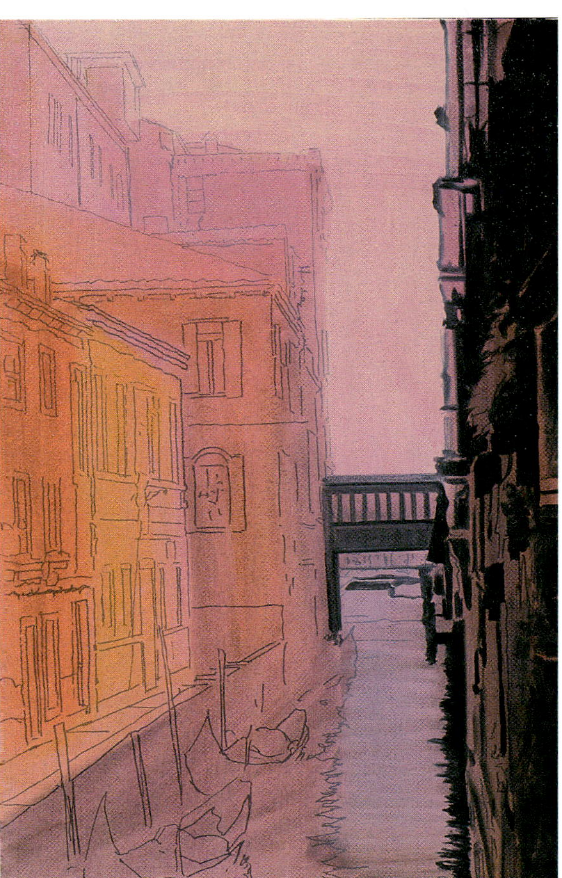

2 Next I use the darkest values (shown above) to define the architectural details, mixing them first with my palette knife. Then, beginning with the buildings at right, I start filling in the outlined shapes with a mixture of sap green, Prussian blue, and alizarin crimson, adding flesh to make a lighter value for variety. I leave some areas unpainted to create negative spaces, which help define the buildings' forms. Then I paint the crossover bridge with mixes of Payne's gray with raw or burnt sienna.

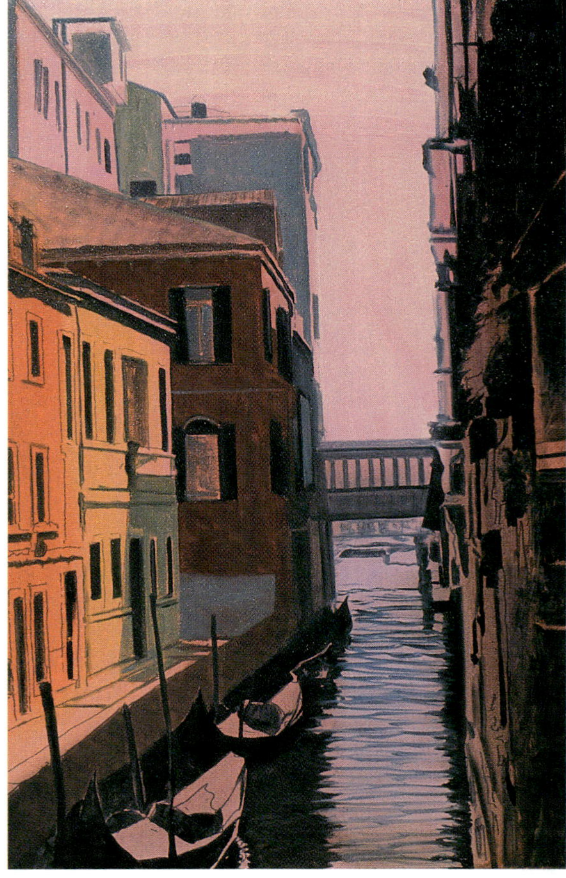

3 Immediately, while the paint on my palette is still wet from the previous step, I continue painting the darkest values on the left. I use a dark reddish mix of Payne's gray, yellow ochre, and phthalo blue for the walls of the center building. Then I maneuver the edge of a medium flat brush to define the windows and doorways, shape the gondolas, and place the horizontal lines of the water reflections. Finally I use cerulean blue to add middle shadow tones at the top of the buildings and to accentuate the ripples on the water.

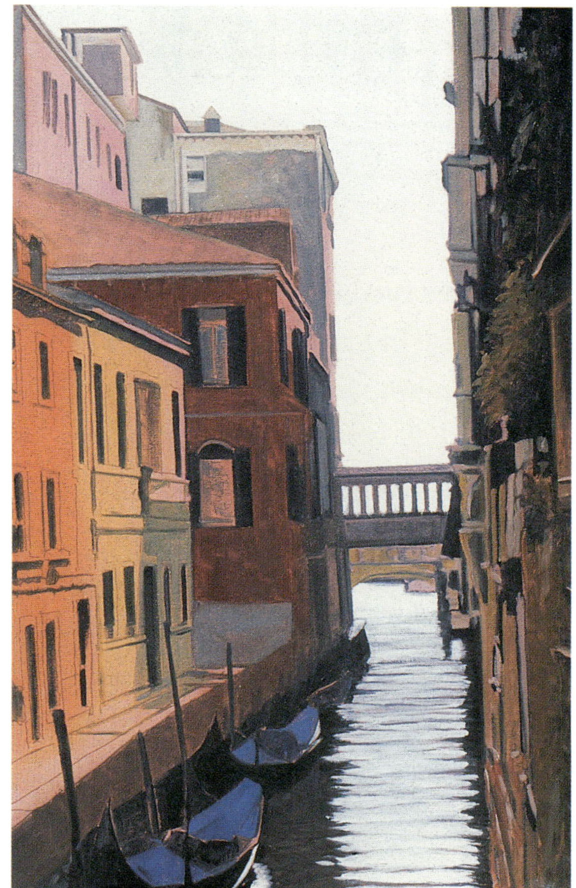

4 Here I add the brightest highlights on the buildings on the left. (See "Light Values" below.) I outline the windows, doorways, and rooflines with light yellows and blues, using the edge of a flat brush. I use the same brush to define the tiles in the rooftops. I work the paint from light to dark, beginning at the tops of the buildings, then adding details to the windows using the lighter gray colors from step three. I also use these colors to lighten the crossover bridge, as objects in the distance usually appear hazier and less defined than do those closer up.

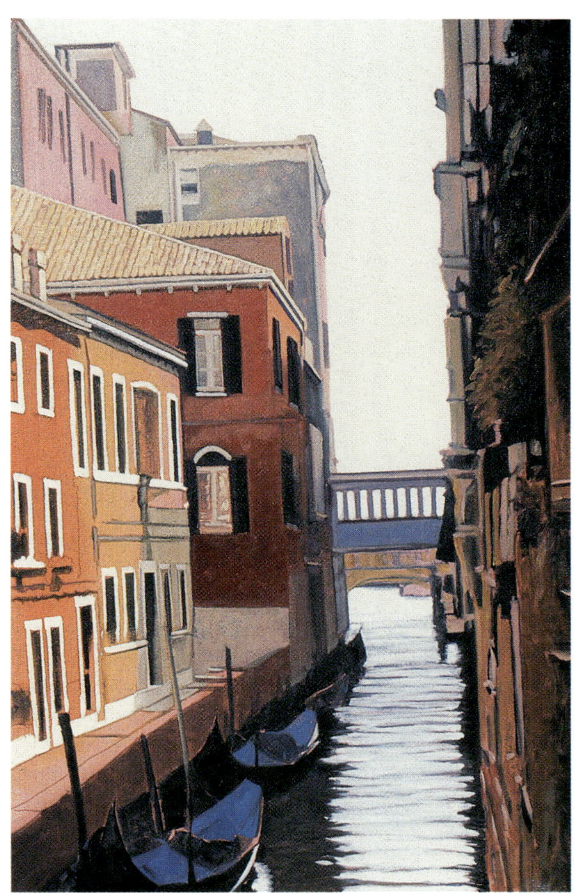

5 Next I mix complementary colors for the building façade details (see "Medium Values" at right) and lighter values for sky and water (see "Light Values"). I add lighter grays to the buildings on the left, defining the separation between the windows and planters on the right. Then I shape the gondolas with cerulean blue. I also add raw sienna and cadmium orange to the buildings on the right. The sky seems to be a solid color, but I create variety by blending blues at the top, then pink, and then yellow where the sky and water meet.

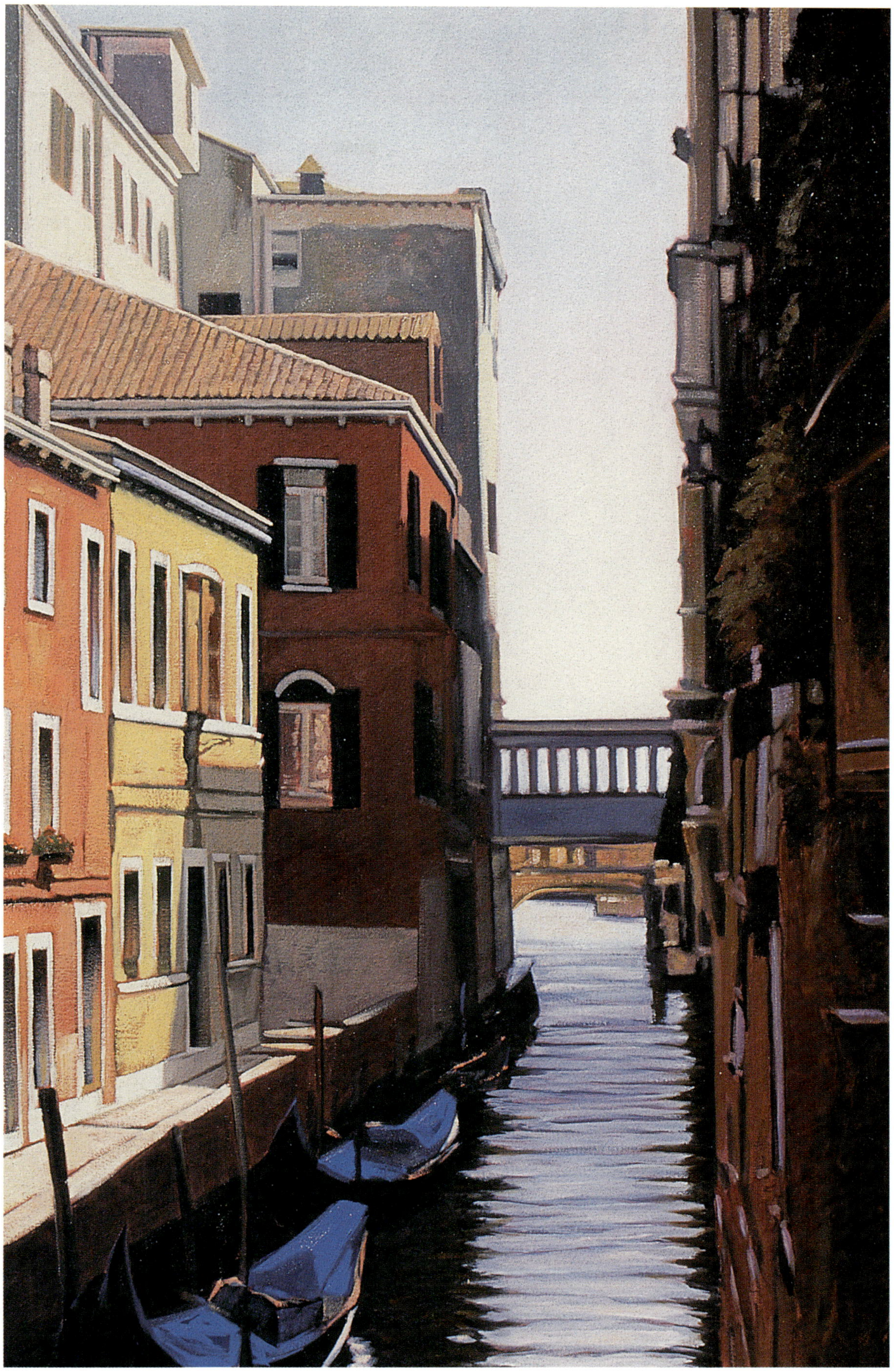

6 Now I mix cadmium red light and cadmium yellow light for the buildings on the left. Then, using cadmium orange mixed with burnt sienna, I create texture by varying the direction of the brushstrokes and paint thickness. I do the same for the yellow building. For the sunlit parts of the buildings, I paint over the areas where the magenta underpainting still shows through, applying white mixed with cadmium orange light and cadmium yellow light. I also brighten the tops of the gondolas with a mix of cerulean blue and white. Finally I add detail to the window boxes using sap green and flesh.

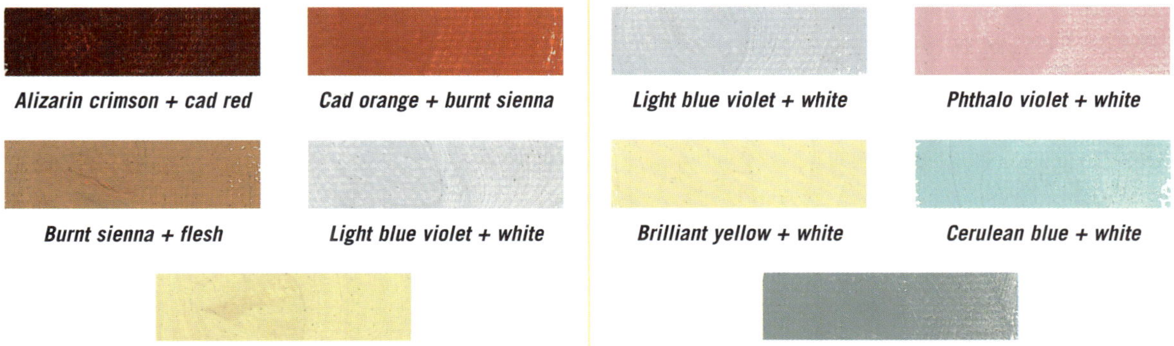

MEDIUM VALUES		LIGHT VALUES	
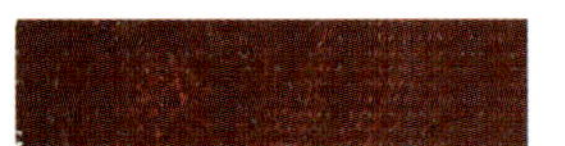	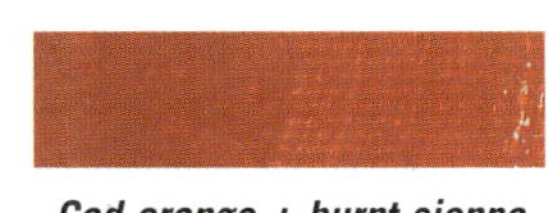		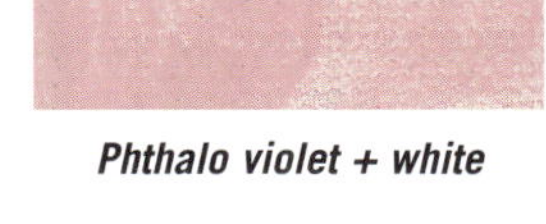
Alizarin crimson + cad red	*Cad orange + burnt sienna*	*Light blue violet + white*	*Phthalo violet + white*
			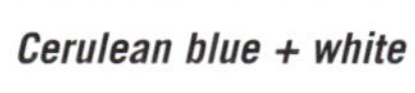
Burnt sienna + flesh	*Light blue violet + white*	*Brilliant yellow + white*	*Cerulean blue + white*

Yellow ochre + white		*Payne's gray + white*	

TELLING A STORY WITH FIGURES

WITH KEITH WICKS

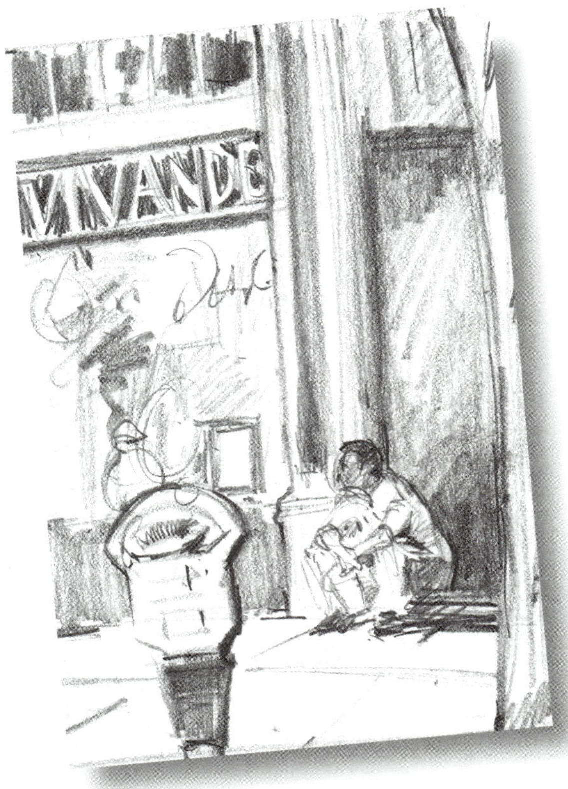

Street scenes can take on an entirely new life with the simple addition of a human figure. In paintings, figures speak through their body language, which can in turn relay a variety of feelings to the viewer, including relaxation, tension, excitement, disinterest, or even attraction. In painting, this nonverbal speech is called "gesture." *Gesture* typically refers to a movement of the body that expresses or emphasizes ideas or emotions, but gesture can also animate a part of the body, such as a finger or an eyebrow. In this painting of a San Francisco street, Keith Wicks uses a figure and the power of gesture to invoke the relaxed feel of break time. The figure's forward-leaning stance, the slump of his posture, and the lift of his head all contribute to the laid-back feeling of the painting—which would be quite different were the figure standing with his hands on hips and looking back into the store!

SKETCHING IN PENCIL I often draw a quick pencil sketch before I begin painting so that I can work out the placement of the elements in my composition. Here the parking meter and window are both of central importance, but the figure is the main focus of the painting; I place him off center to create more interest. At this stage, I also work out the position of the man's body—from the relaxed placement of his elbows on his knees to his turned-away gaze.

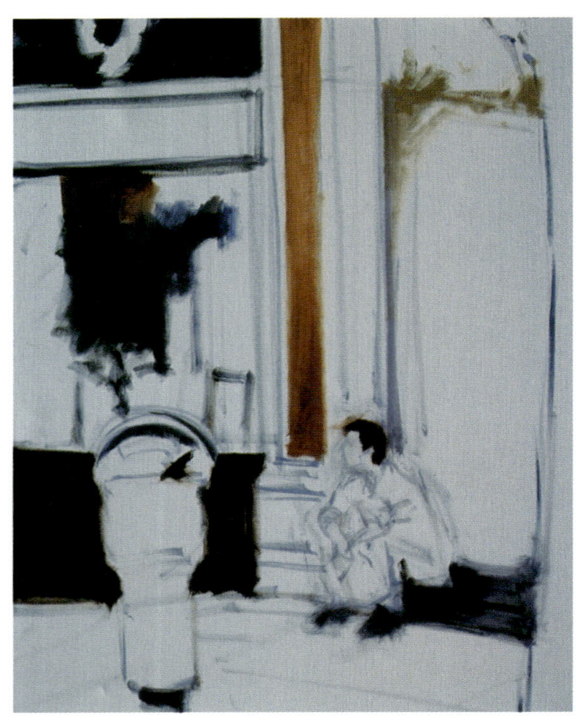

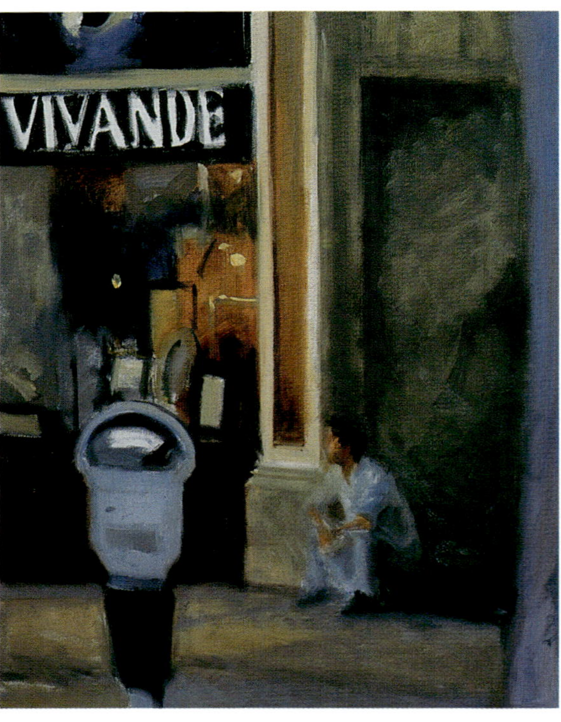

1 I begin my painting on an untoned canvas, drawing with a flat brush and ultramarine blue thinned with medium. (I use a cool blue because it will provide contrast to the warm tones I add later.) I lay in the dark values first, all thinned with solvent. With a mix of ultramarine blue, alizarin crimson, and sap green, I paint the upper left window and form the shadows below the chef's feet and on the stoop. Then I paint the building wall with alizarin brown madder, adding the ultramarine blue mix along the lower edge. I mix alizarin crimson with a bit of sap green for the color inside the window. Then I create the vertical stripe on the building with Indian yellow, yellow ochre, and a touch of alizarin brown madder. I indicate the doorway depth with raw sienna.

2 Now, still working with the flat brush, I block in the doorway using a wash of raw sienna mixed with ultramarine blue. Within the doorway panel, I add a full range of warm browns, all grayed with ultramarine blue. Then, to shape the sidewalk, I apply yellow ochre mixed with raw sienna, shading the lower portion of the sidewalk with dioxazine violet that has been slightly grayed with yellow ochre. To create the base of the cement column—located next to the chef—I mix raw sienna with white, adding a touch of ultramarine blue. I also want to create a sense of luminosity within the window, so I paint in patches of thinned Indian yellow mixed with alizarin brown.

3 Next I want to develop values that push back my darker areas and bring forward the lighter objects of interest. First I darken the doorway with Payne's gray. Then I clothe the chef with ultramarine blue and white, adding a touch of the ultramarine blue, alizarin crimson, and sap green mix down his side. I use the same mix to shape the parking meter, adding white for the grays that lighten the sidewalk. I form the chef's arms and face with a mix of alizarin crimson, Indian yellow, and transparent alizarin brown, cooled with a touch of blue under the chin. The facial highlights are a mix of cadmium red, Indian yellow, and white, with less white toward the nose. Within the window, I block in the shapes of the objects without too much definition.

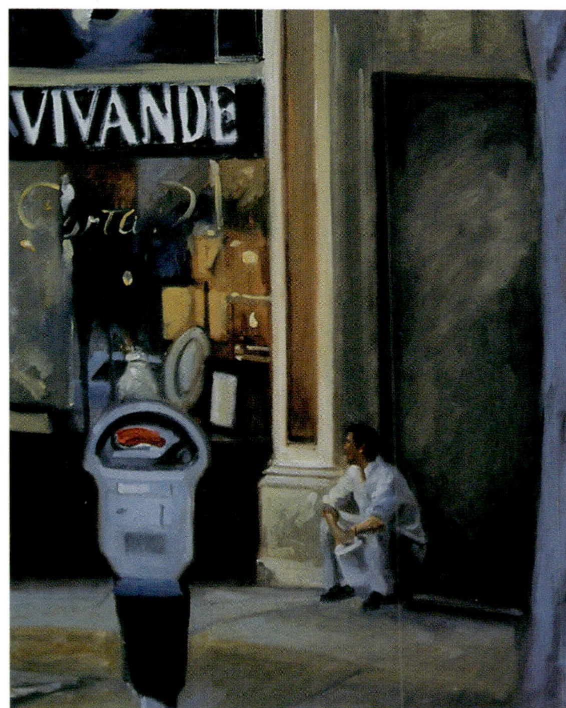

4 I color the tree trunk at the painting's far right edge with alizarin crimson, ultramarine blue, and white, adding a bit of the ultramarine blue, alizarin crimson, and sap green mixture to indicate the tree bark. Two strokes of red give life to the meter: First I stroke alizarin crimson mixed with cadmium red; then I lay straight cadmium on top of that. I work in Indian yellow and titanium white to create partial letters that represent a reflection visible on the window. Then I shape the restaurant sign by painting around what will be the final letters with the ultramarine blue, alizarin crimson, and sap green mixture.

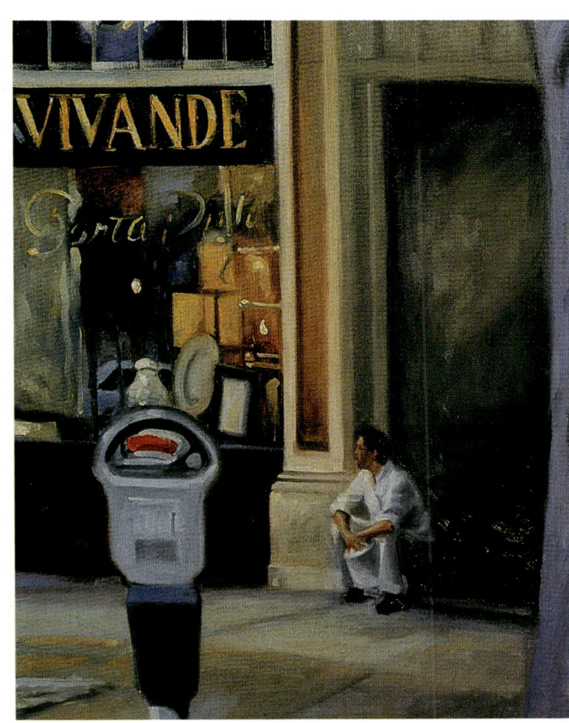

5 Now I mix white with Indian yellow to color the restaurant sign. I separate the panes above the sign with strokes of ochre and white toned with gray. I define the chef's arms with additional values of cadmium red, Indian yellow, and titanium white. Then I develop the chef's back and his shoes and clothing by adding darker values. In each step, I deepen the doorway behind the chef to create more contrast and to bring a stronger focus to the chef. Next I lighten and thicken all areas of the concrete and define the seams in the concrete with dark gray lines.

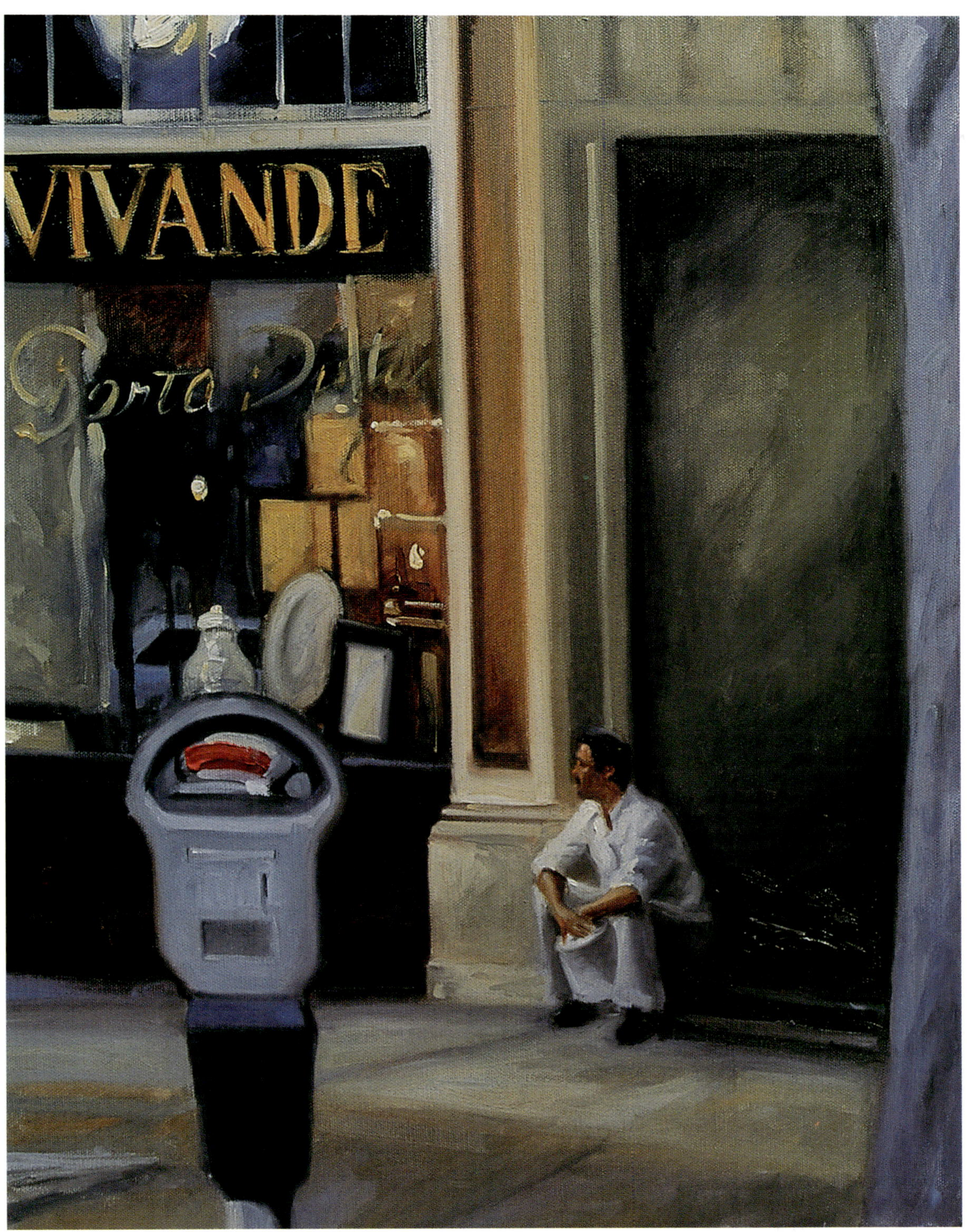

6 Now all that is needed are quick touches and final adjustments. I correct the upper window panes so the objects within are less distracting. I also refine all the lettering. Next I continue to darken the top of the doorway so that it recedes farther. I use highlights to make it seem as if the chef's face is turned slightly more toward the sun; then I shift the ear to the right, add a moustache, and darken the hair. To finish, I add detail to the meter, defining shapes and accentuating the darks.

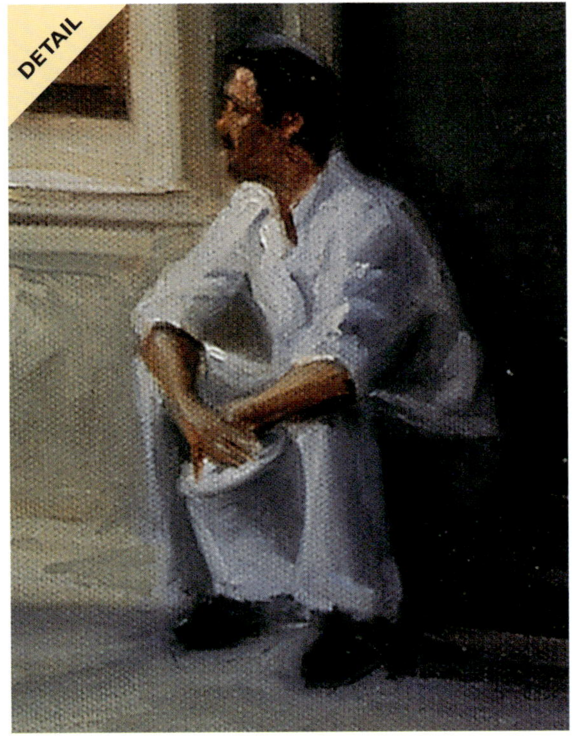

◄ CLOSEUP VIEW This detail image shows you a closer view of the chef, allowing you to more clearly see the brushstrokes and colors used. Notice where the highlights are placed and how simply but effectively the figure is rendered with a minimum of well-placed strokes. You may want to use this closeup to help you practice, before you try your hand at the final painting. Careful observation and a lot of practice are the keys to successful paintings.

Contrasting Values

WITH KEITH WICKS

The eye is naturally drawn toward light values, so objects painted in lighter colors often naturally "pop" forward in a scene. Incorporating light values in your composition is a great way to lead the eye around the painting and to bring attention to the focal point. And pairing contrasting elements in a scene—such as light colors against a dark background—can intensify the effect of the light values, producing even more eye-catching results. For this New Orleans street, Keith Wicks sets the stage for drama by choosing a white horse for his focal point. The horse would draw the eye against nearly any colored backdrop; but the dark background colors Keith uses provide a stark and striking contrast, immediately drawing the eye to the white horse and establishing it as the unquestionable center of interest.

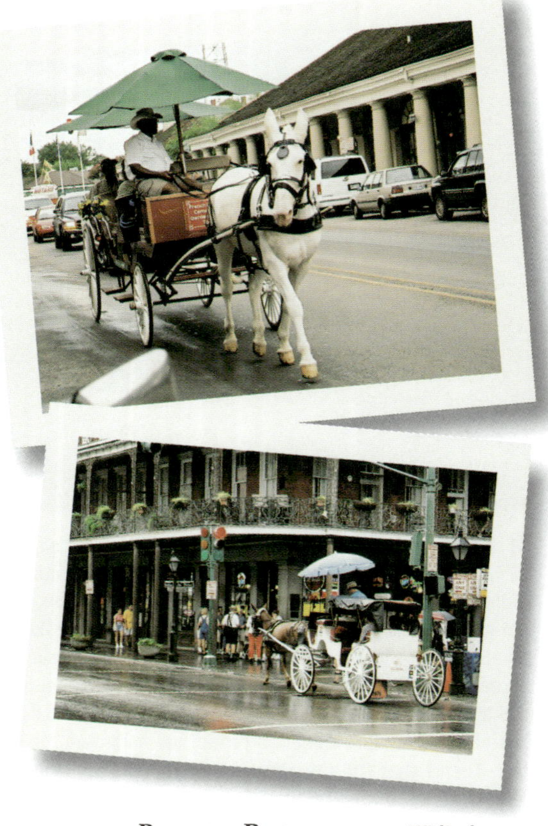

COLOR PALETTE

alizarin crimson, alizarin violet lake, cadmium red medium, cadmium yellow deep, French ultramarine blue, raw sienna, sap green, titanium white, yellow ochre

DARK BACKGROUND COLORS

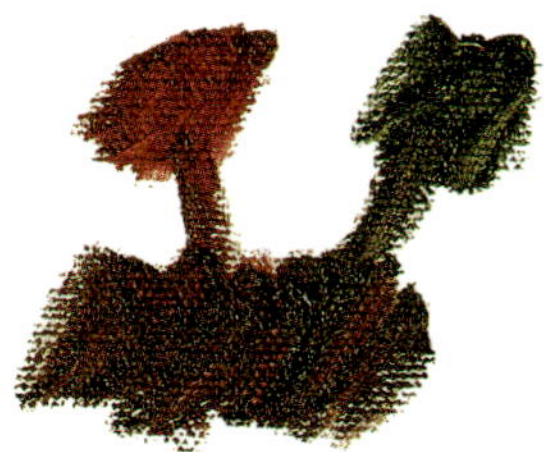

Alizarin crimson + sap green

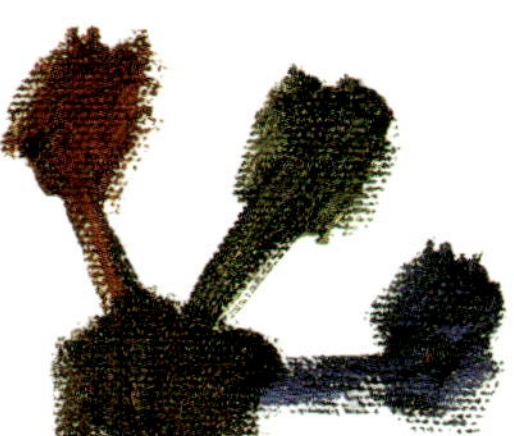

Alizarin crimson + sap green + ultramarine blue

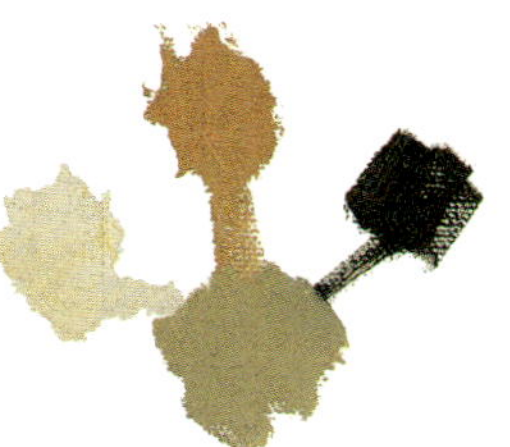

Titanium white + yellow ochre + deep black mix

COMBINING PHOTO RESOURCES While in New Orleans, I was immediately attracted to the horse-drawn carriages. But the muted background where I spotted the white horse didn't do the image justice. By combining references and setting the horse against the dark, wet backdrop of a city street, I was able to create a scene containing contrast, drama, and interest.

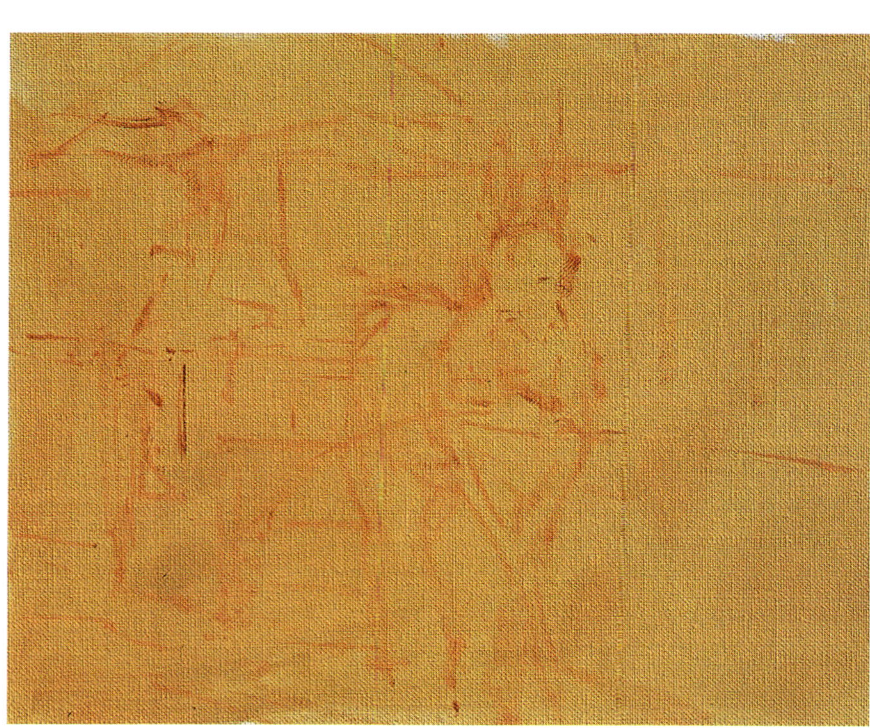

1 First I tone my canvas with a warm wash of yellow ochre thinned with odorless mineral spirits, laying down a contrast for the cooler colors of my final painting. After this dries, I begin "drawing" the subject with raw sienna, creating a series of dots and dashes with a small brush. There is no need for a complete sketch because, as I move through the painting process, my image may undergo adjustments. I need only a simple guideline for now, which leaves me free to make changes later.

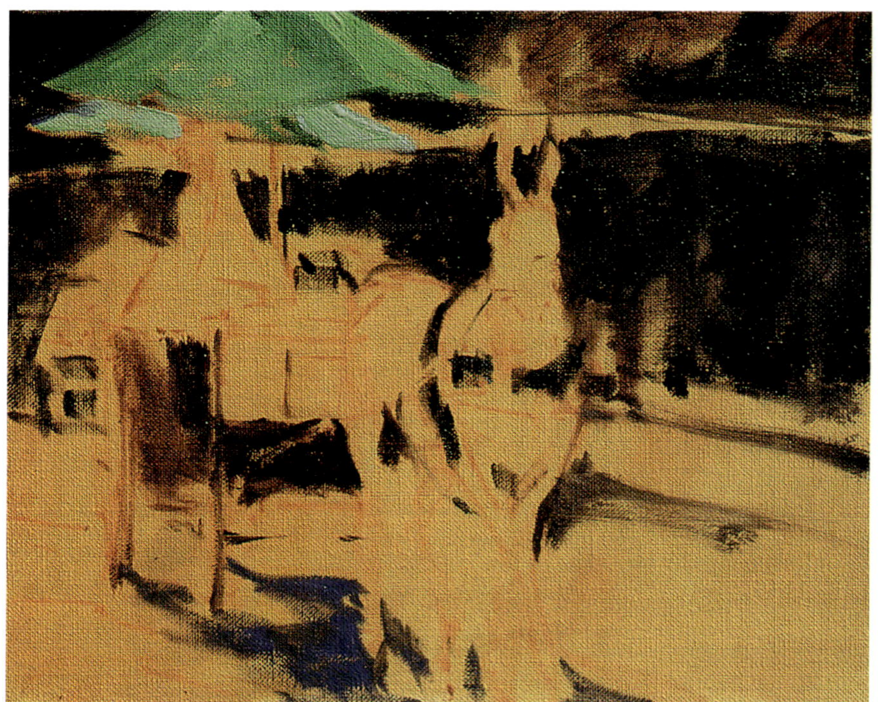

2 Now I block in areas of color using a large round brush. (A large bright will also work.) Working with darker colors first, I refer to my photos as I apply intense but thin layers of color, beginning with a mix of alizarin crimson and French ultramarine blue for the dark background. To add warmth to some areas of the upper background, I apply sap green mixed with alizarin crimson. (See the color samples above.) I also block in the shape of the umbrellas with viridian green, painting loosely to allow the warm ochre to peek through.

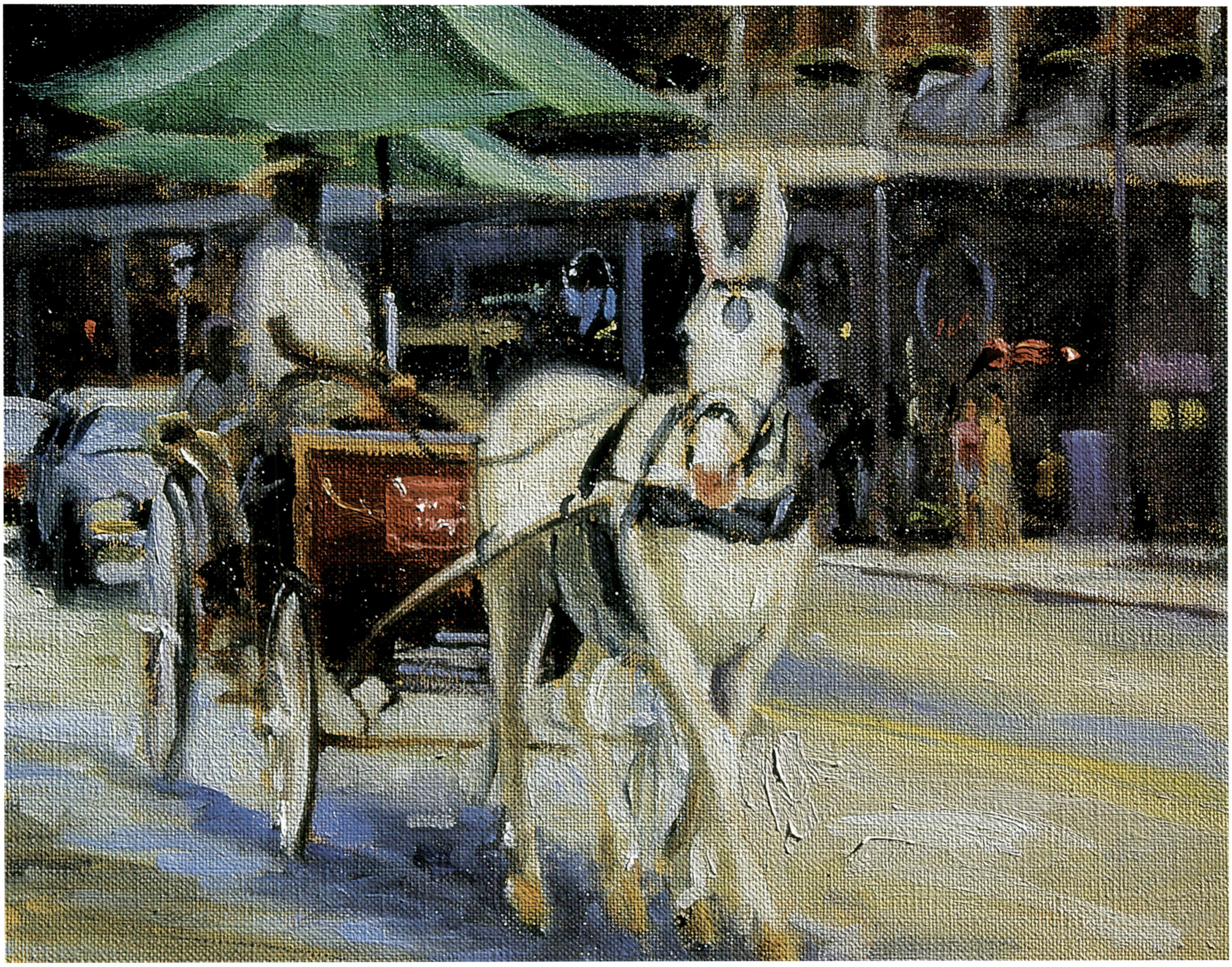

5 With a medium sable brush, I apply final highlights and a few details. I add the horse's hooves and reins, the wagon wheels, the automobiles, and the detail on the background balcony. I avoid overworking the painting because I want the warm undercolors to continue to show through, providing a sense of harmony to the entire scene. At this point, I know I'm finished working because the painting matches the vision I had when I set out to capture the energy and fresh excitement of a cool New Orleans day.

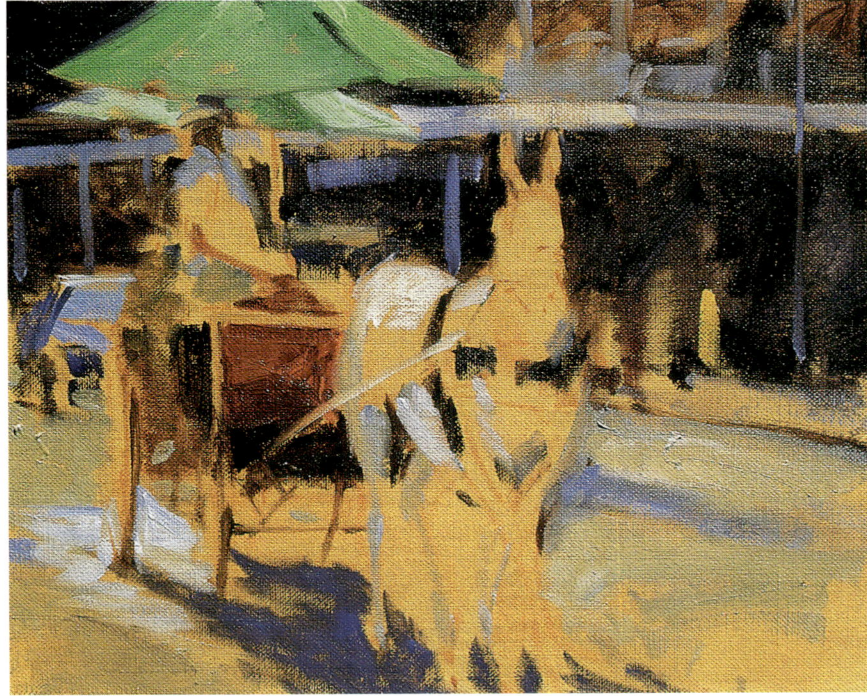

3 At this point, colors are less important than the values, which establish depth. As I move around the canvas, I check the neighboring values to determine the strength and placement of my darks. For the deep brown color of the under-carriage, I mix alizarin crimson, French ultramarine blue, and sap green. I began layering with transparent colors, but now I use thicker, opaque applications that lead toward a more finished look. Even now, the toned canvas peeks through much of the blocked-in color, producing a sense of vibrancy.

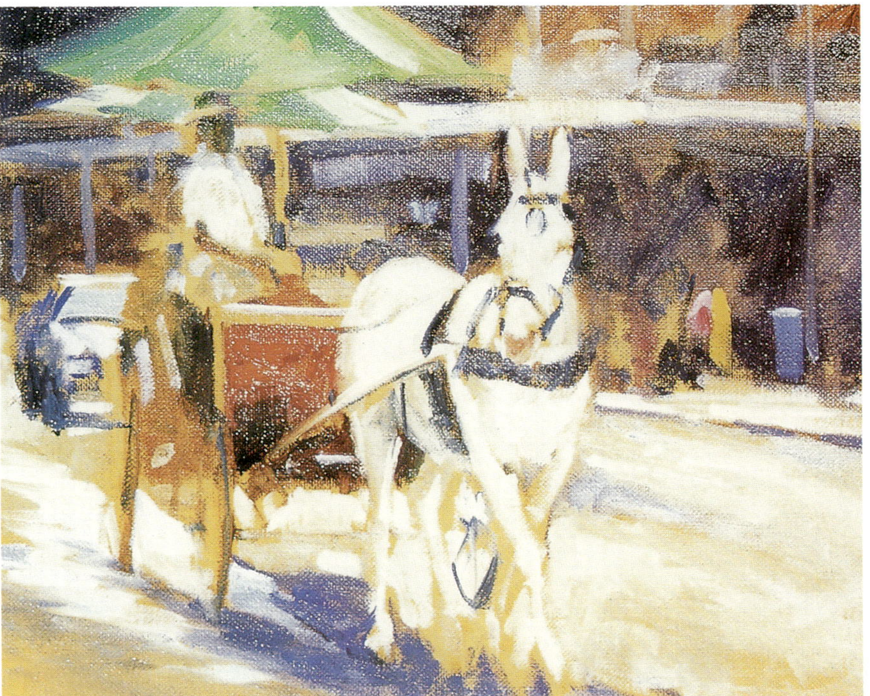

4 I continue to check the balance of values and colors as I develop the detail areas. I am now using a combination of small round, flat, and bright brushes and working with more opaque colors to tighten the image. I capture the sunlight on the umbrella with a combination of viridian green, titanium white, and cadmium yellow medium. Then I deliver a colorful punch of cadmium red medium to the horse buggy. A mixture of titanium white and French ultramarine blue gives form to both the horse and the wet road.

Working with a Limited Palette

with Keith Wicks

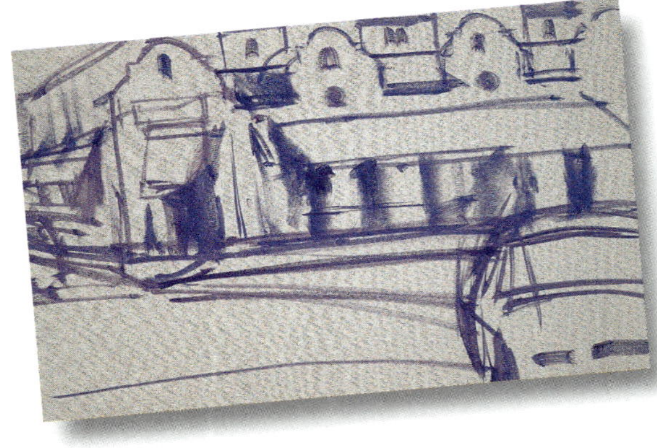

SKETCHING WITH PAINT **Because the color palette I've selected is full of dark and shadowy colors, I've deliberately left my canvas untoned to maintain a sense of brightness. I create my initial sketch by drawing on the untoned canvas with a brush and thinned dioxazine violet, a dominant color in my limited, cool-toned palette.**

COLOR PALETTE

alizarin crimson, cadmium red, cadmium yellow deep, cerulean blue, dioxazine violet, Indian red, Indian yellow, sap green, titanium white, ultramarine blue, yellow ochre

An artist may choose to use a *limited palette* (just a few colors) for convenience, experimentation, or the desire to express a particular mood in a scene (such as using only reds and oranges to evoke the feeling of danger). Working with a limited palette can also force you to think creatively—you must plan your values and blend your colors to produce enough variations to both establish harmony and create contrast in your painting. It's certainly acceptable to depict a street scene using a large selection of colors; but, contrary to what you might think, working with a limited palette can allow you a greater degree of expression, as many of the paintings in this book demonstrate. Here Keith Wicks employs subtle variations in color to produce the "feel" of a cool morning in Sonoma, California. Even while limiting his painting to a palette of mostly cool blues and grays, Keith is able to imbue this street scene with a sense of deserted calm, quiet, and stillness.

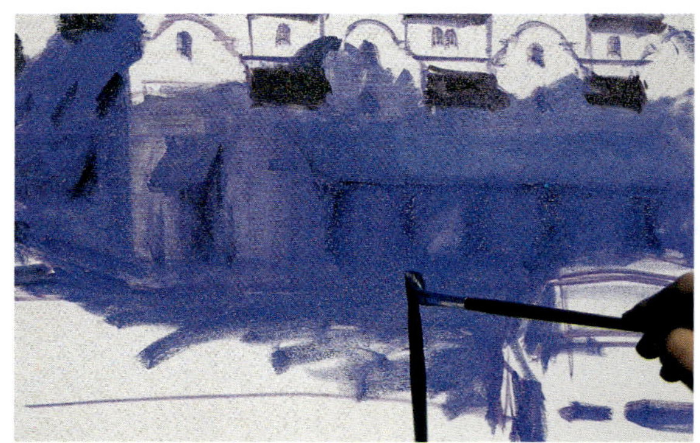

1 After sketching in the basic composition and establishing clear guidelines for the architectural detail, I continue working with dioxazine violet and a medium bristle brush, blocking in some of the dark values and shadows.

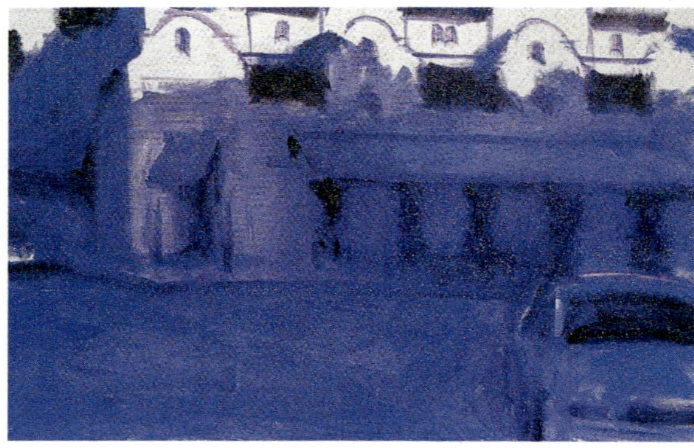

2 With the same brush, I create a dark, thin wash of ultramarine blue mixed with violet and thinner. Then I fill in the shadow areas, including the car and the recessed areas of the windows and doorways.

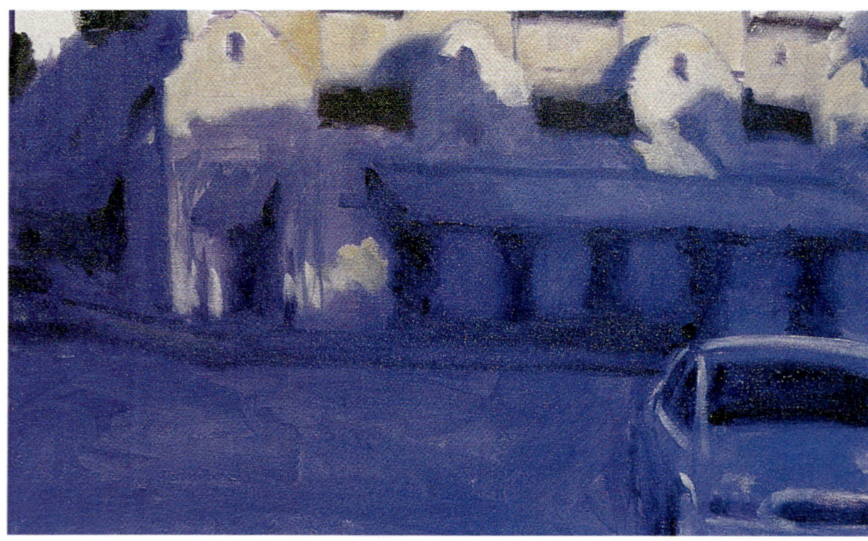

3 After adding a bit more blue to the ultramarine blue and violet mix, I fill in the larger areas of cast shadows on the building. For the left side of the building, I apply a darker value to lend depth and dimension to the scene. I fill in the shape of the two trees on the upper left using a blend of thinned sap green and ultramarine blue. Now the process of laying in the shadow areas is complete.

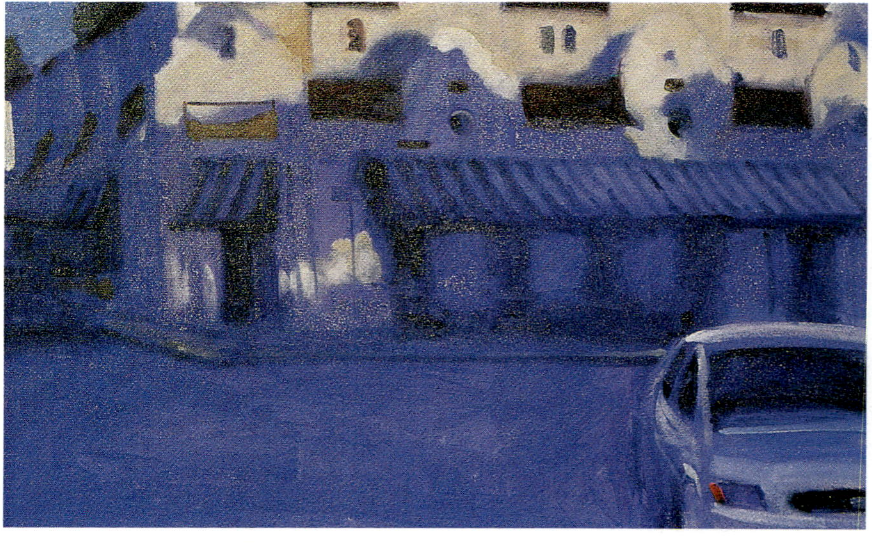

4 Next my objective is to emphasize the warm sunlight filtering through the trees onto the top of the building, creating a stark contrast that adds drama to the painting. First I introduce Indian red mixed with ultramarine blue and dioxazine violet to block in the roof areas. Then I add the sunlit areas of the building with a mix of titanium white, yellow ochre, and cadmium yellow.

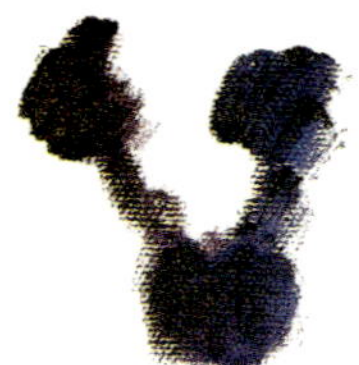

DARK SHADOWS
Dioxazine violet + ultramarine blue

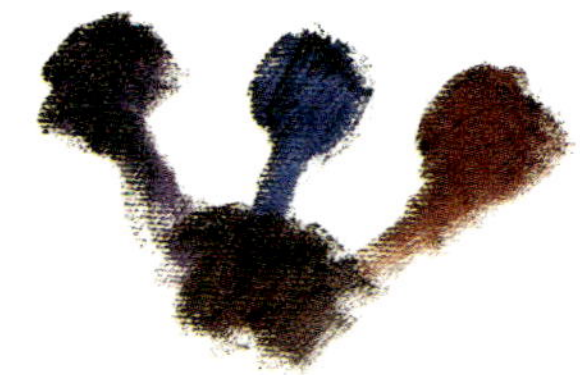

ROOF DARKS
Dioxazine violet + ultramarine blue + Indian red

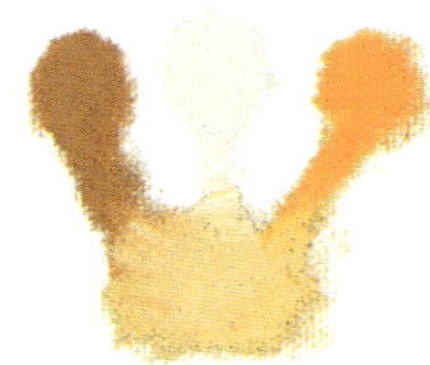

SUNLIT BUILDING
Titanium white + yellow ochre + cadmium yellow deep

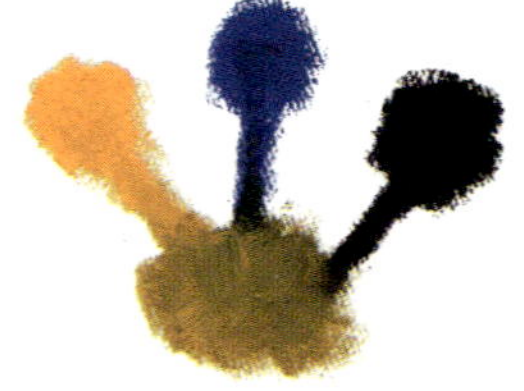

SIGN DARKS
Cadmium yellow deep + ultramarine blue + dioxazine violet

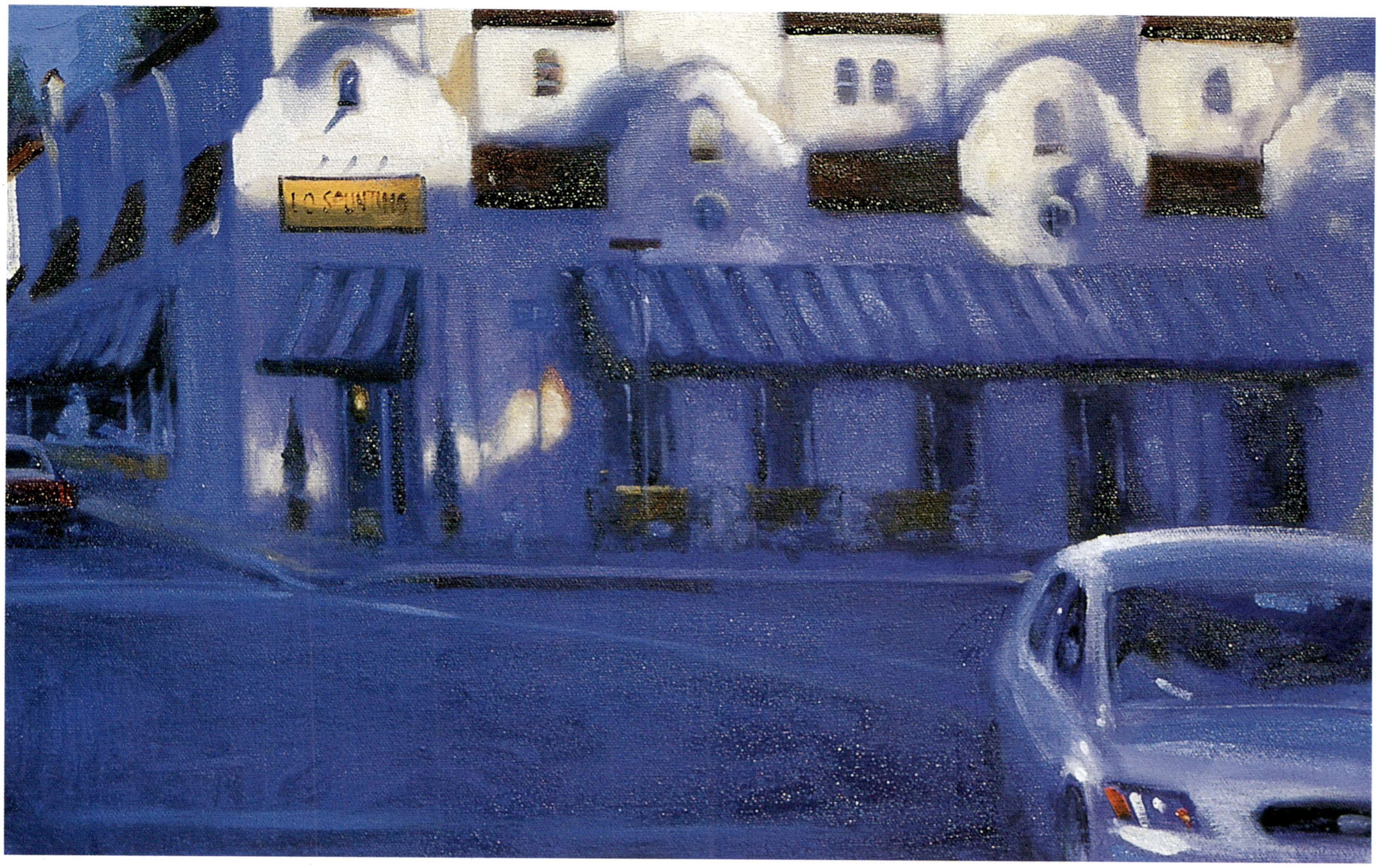

7 I use a thin sable brush with violet and Indian red to paint the sign name, slightly indicating the letters rather than fully rendering them. Next I bathe the building in warm sunlight using titanium white and a bit of Indian yellow. I add yellow ochre to the mix to vary the temperature before painting the area of dappled sunlight, which is caused by the shifting light passing through branches of the tree. For the finishing details, I touch in highlights on the car's headlamps, using straight white for some and a mix of cadmium red and cadmium yellow deep for others.

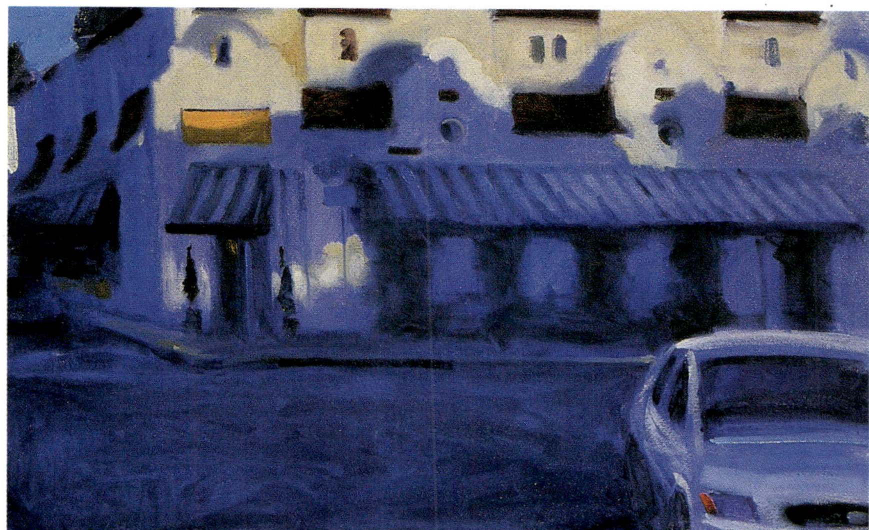

5 For the sky, I apply a thinned cerulean blue, painting right up to the edge of the building so that no white canvas shows. Next I mix cadmium yellow deep into the blue and violet mixture and paint the shadowed sign over the doorway. Then I introduce titanium white to the blue and violet mix, warming the color by adding more violet; I use this mix to cover the shadow areas more opaquely. On the left side of the building, I indicate reflected light using a mix of white, ultramarine blue, and a touch of violet to cool the shadow.

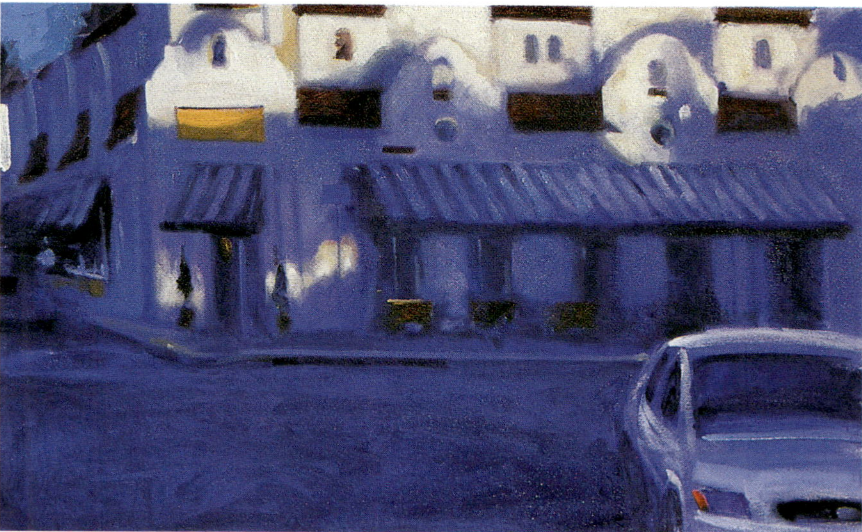

6 I switch to a medium bright brush now, which lends more control as I move and correct shapes within the shadow areas. I use a fresh mix of ultramarine blue and dioxazine violet to indicate the stripes on the awnings, varying the width by manipulating the brush angle. I also further develop the car with this mix. Then I add the lighted portion of the sign above the entry using an intense cadmium yellow deep. With a small bristle brush, I dab highlights on the car using a thick mix of white with a small amount of ultramarine blue. I paint the window boxes with a yellow ochre added to the blue and violet mix. Next I punch up the darks, adding sap green, alizarin crimson, and ultramarine blue to the door and windows.

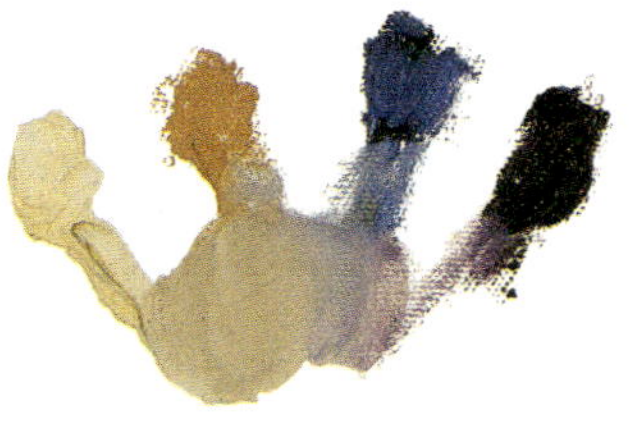

MID-TONE SHADOWS
Titanium white + yellow ochre + ultramarine blue + dioxazine violet

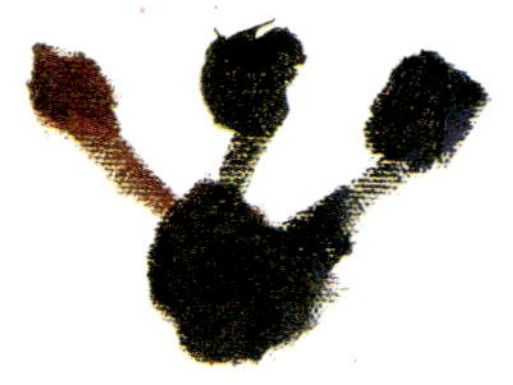

DARKEST SHADOWS
Alizarin crimson + sap green + ultramarine blue

HEIGHTENING PERSPECTIVE

WITH MICHAEL OBERMEYER

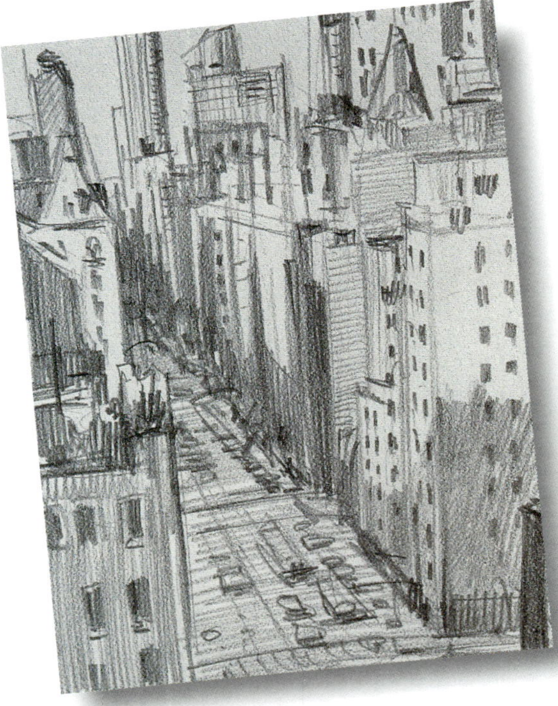

Although many aspects contribute to realistic paintings, nothing will make your street scenes appear more true-to-life than a good understanding of perspective. *Perspective* is essentially the representation of objects in three-dimensional space to give the illusion of distance and depth. In other words, perspective is what makes objects—and the space between objects—appear to get smaller as they recede into the distance. Perspective is a complex concept, but you probably already know more about it than you think! For example, if you've ever observed the way the lines of a road seem to converge to a dot far off in the distance, you've witnessed the effect of *linear perspective*.

Perspective is especially important when your street scene includes buildings, such as the towering skyscrapers in Michael Obermeyer's painting of New York City's Madison Avenue. Michael chose a high, aerial point of view for a painting that accentuates depth and distance. From this extreme viewpoint, three planes are involved, each with their own receding lines (see the box below), contributing to a heightened sense of drama.

CHOOSING A VIEWPOINT I recommend always traveling with a sketchbook and pencils. An extra ten minutes or an unexpected wait may present itself. This exciting view of Madison Avenue was visible from a hotel window. With sketchbook handy, I was able to capture a rare viewpoint, recording the essentials about perspective that I would need to complete a dynamic painting later.

COLOR PALETTE

alizarin crimson, cadmium yellow light, cerulean blue, raw umber, titanium white, ultramarine blue

UNDERSTANDING PERSPECTIVE

To give the illusion of depth and distance, artists must draw all the elements in their compositions in the correct perspective; elements closer to the viewer will be larger than those in the distance. Perspective can be applied to one plane, two planes, or even three; but in every case, the receding lines of all the objects will appear to converge at one or more points on the *horizon line*—the line at the viewer's eye level. The points where the lines converge are called the "vanishing points." If the lines are on one plane, as with railroad tracks or a row of trees, the receding lines converge at one vanishing point; this is called "one-point perspective." (See the diagram below left.) If two planes are involved, such as a house viewed from one corner, each plane has its own vanishing point; this is called "two-point perspective." (See the diagram below right.) From extreme high and low viewpoints—called "bird's eye" and "worm's eye" points of view—there are two vanishing points for the horizontal lines and a third for the vertical lines. With paper, a pencil and a ruler in hand, practice drawing different scenes from different perspectives. Your paintings will benefit greatly from your understanding of the basics.

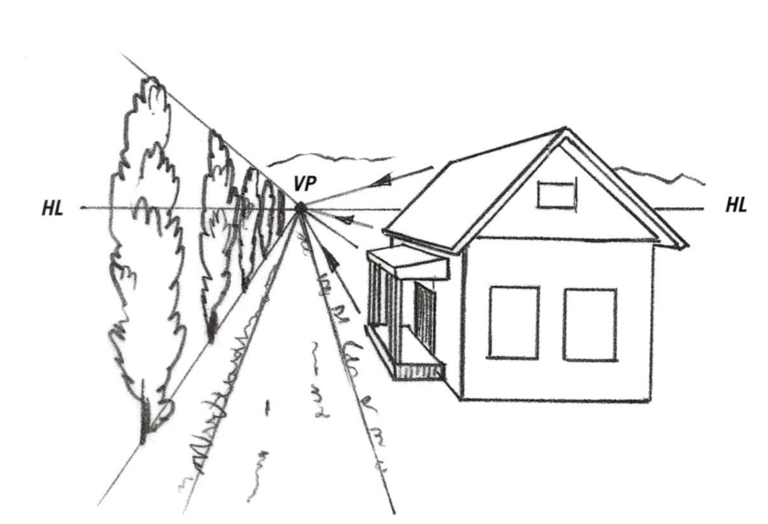

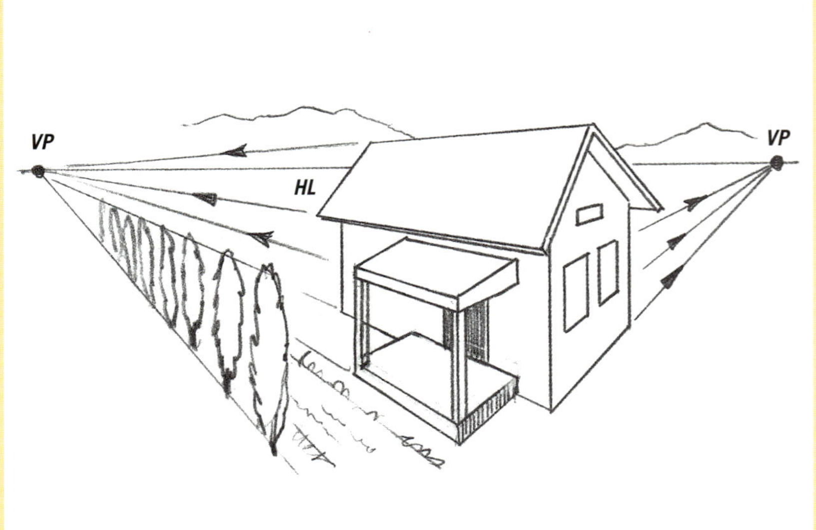

ONE-POINT PERSPECTIVE In this drawing, the guidelines show that all the lines of the house, the road, and the trees recede into the distance until they converge at a single vanishing point (VP) on the horizon line (HL). The side of the building facing us is the closest plane to us. Its bottom and top edges are parallel to the horizon line, and its vertical sides are parallel to the vertical edges of the picture plane. The left side of the building appears to recede, so the lines continue the angles of the roof, eave, base of the house, and porch out to the vanishing point.

TWO-POINT PERSPECTIVE In this drawing, the corner of the building is the closest part to us, and the two sides recede to two different vanishing points on the horizon. These vanishing points do not necessarily have to be on the drawing (and most often they are not, because if they're too close together, the objects drawn will look distorted). When you draw, place a straightedge on any line on the house (windows and porch too), and continue it to one of the vanishing points to make sure the perspective is correct. Your dexterity with these visual cues will help you create depth and dimension in your work.

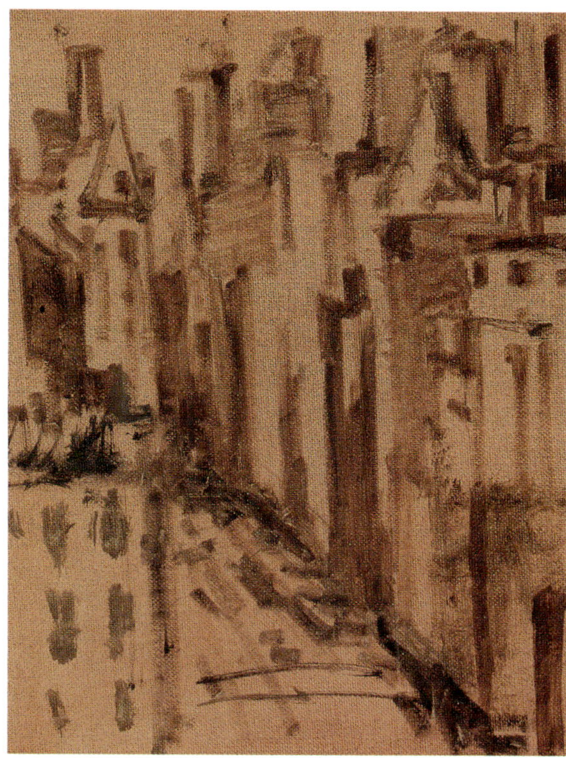  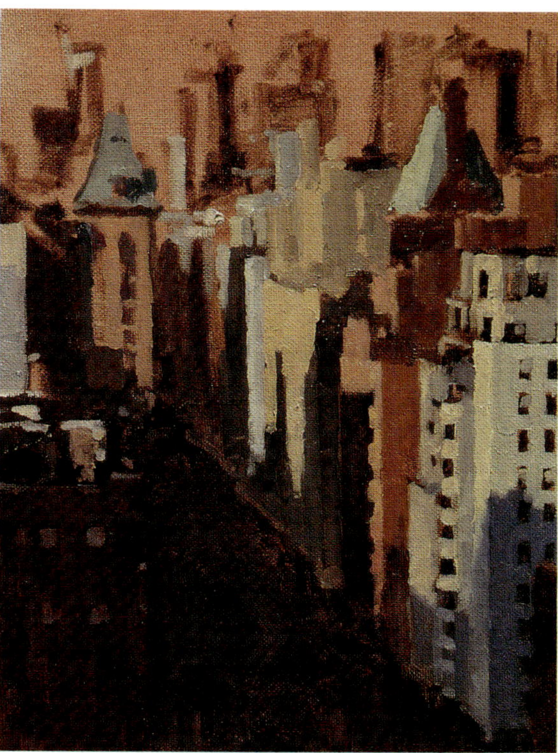

1 Because this subject has so many dark areas, I begin by toning the canvas with a warm neutral color—yellow ochre. This undertone will lend warmth to the dark values I add later and keep them from becoming too dull or flat. Next I loosely sketch the composition on the toned canvas, using a wash of raw umber. I thin the wash to rework parts of the sketch where necessary.

2 Now, using a large, flat sable brush, I block in the dark areas with a thin mix of alizarin crimson, ultramarine blue, and raw umber. I try to keep the colors in this painting warm—not too purple or blue—to replicate the warmth of the sunlit cityscape. I vary the color temperature in the contrasting shadows by adjusting the amount of blue or raw umber I use.

3 Next I begin to build up the light areas, establishing texture by applying the paint thickly with a medium flat bristle brush. Because I want my lighter shapes to be warm in temperature, I mix a little cadmium yellow light into most of my colors to create harmony. As I paint, I compare the light colors to one another and to the dark shapes, adjusting the colors for balance.

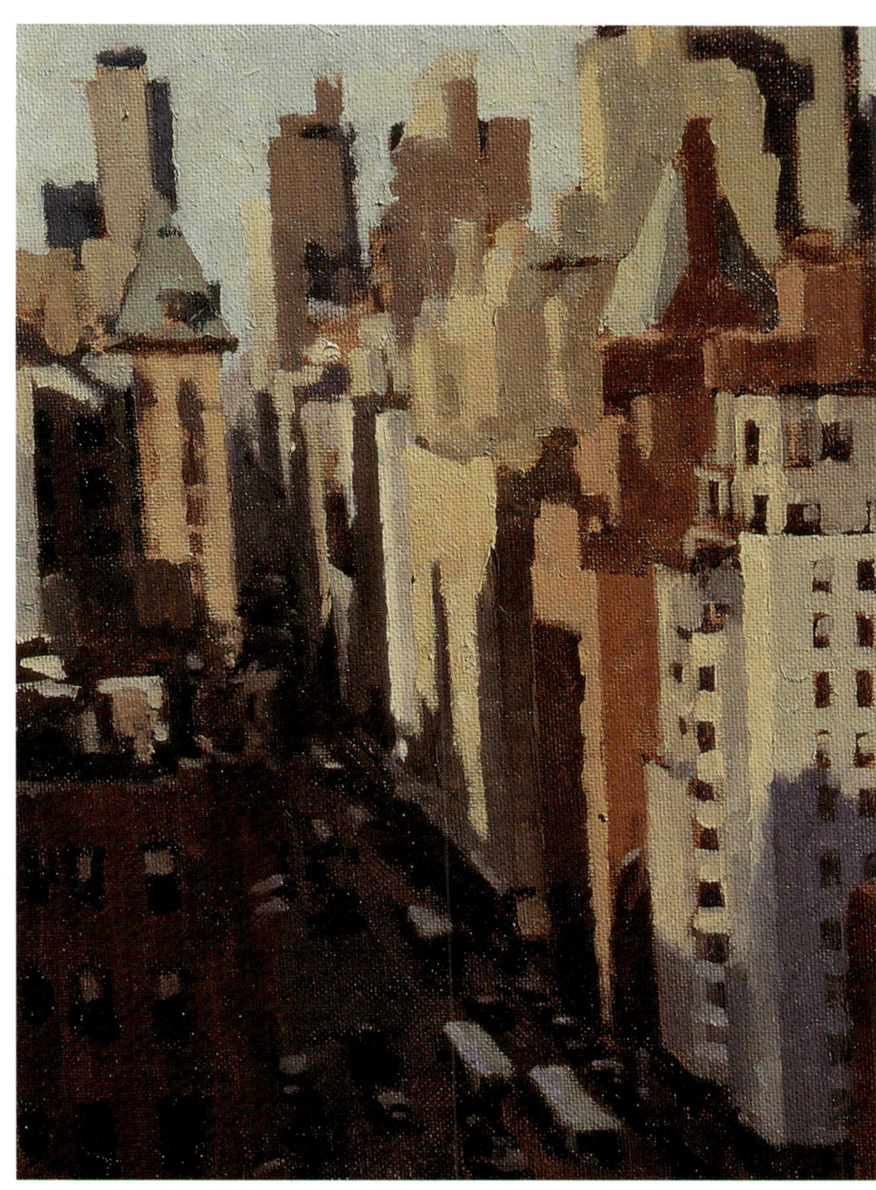 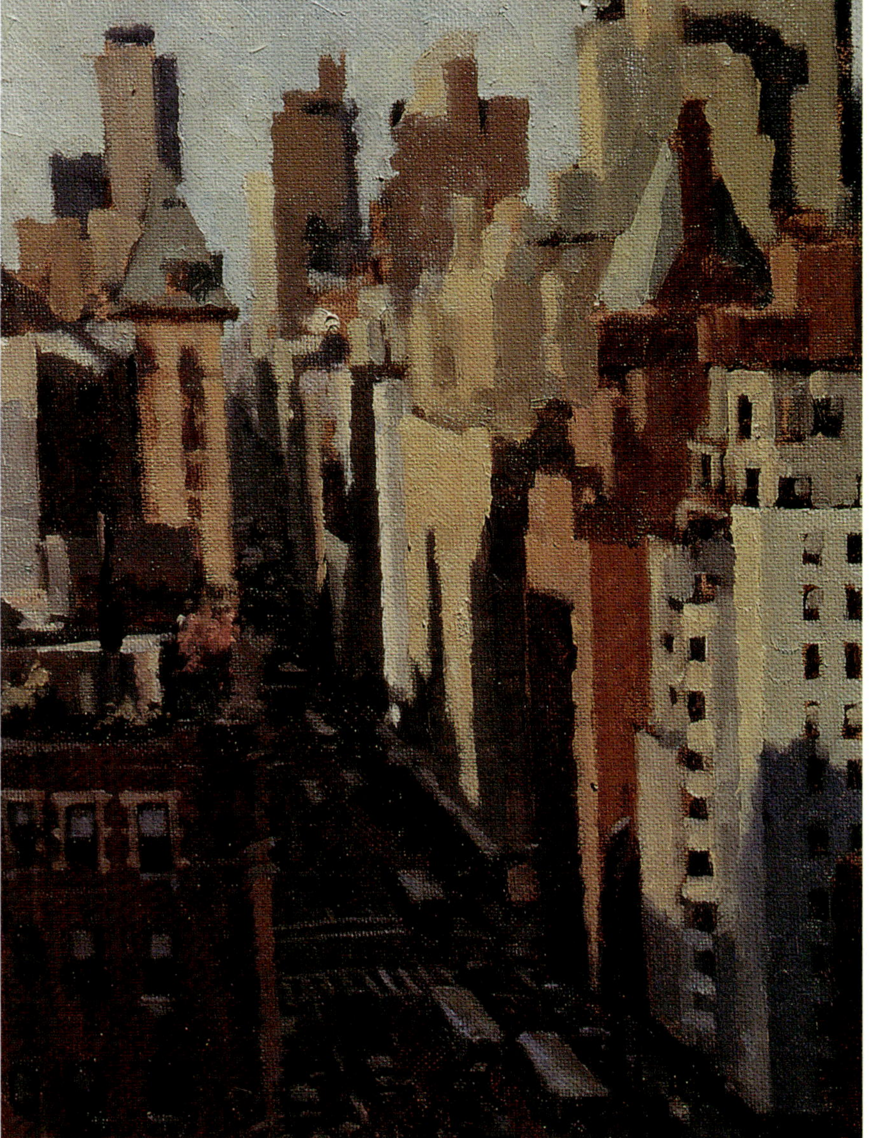

4 After blocking in the simple skyline shapes, I paint the sky with a warm mix of cerulean blue, a very small amount of cadmium yellow light, and liberal amounts of titanium white. Again I thickly apply the paint, using a medium flat bristle brush, which can hold a lot of paint. Like the buildings, the sky has a warm tone and—at this stage—it appears almost green. I also start to paint smaller shapes in the street below, indicating buses and cars. As before, I create the darker shapes first and then the lighter shapes.

5 I continue adding details to the street using small flat and round brushes. I also begin to develop more detail on the foreground building, using all the mixed colors now on my palette. With a complex composition like this, it's important for me to remain loose. Instead of producing a perfect replica of each structure with exact angles, I simply create the suggestion of buildings, not an exact window-for-window re-creation. I use simple dabs of paint to establish the feel of this urban landscape.

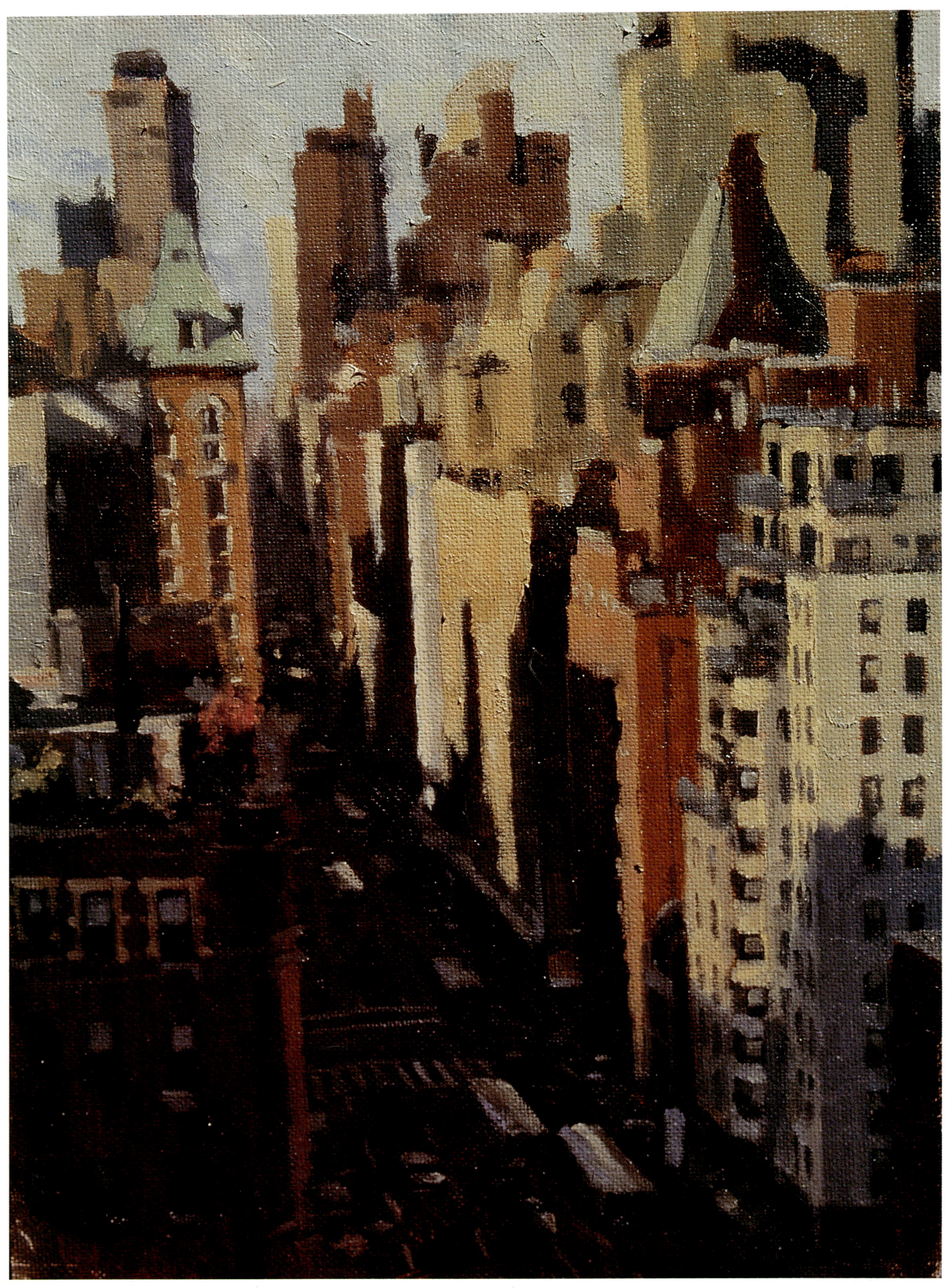

6 At this point, I settle into a rhythm while adding details to the buildings, painting smaller light and dark shapes within the larger shapes. I use small flat brushes to apply thicker paint in the lighter areas and thinner paint for the darker areas. I redraw shapes occasionally to keep the initial composition that I had in the sketch. I also adjust my values throughout, making sure the lights and darks are accurate. Now I am ready to hone in on the remaining details with a very small flat or round brush (or even a rigger).

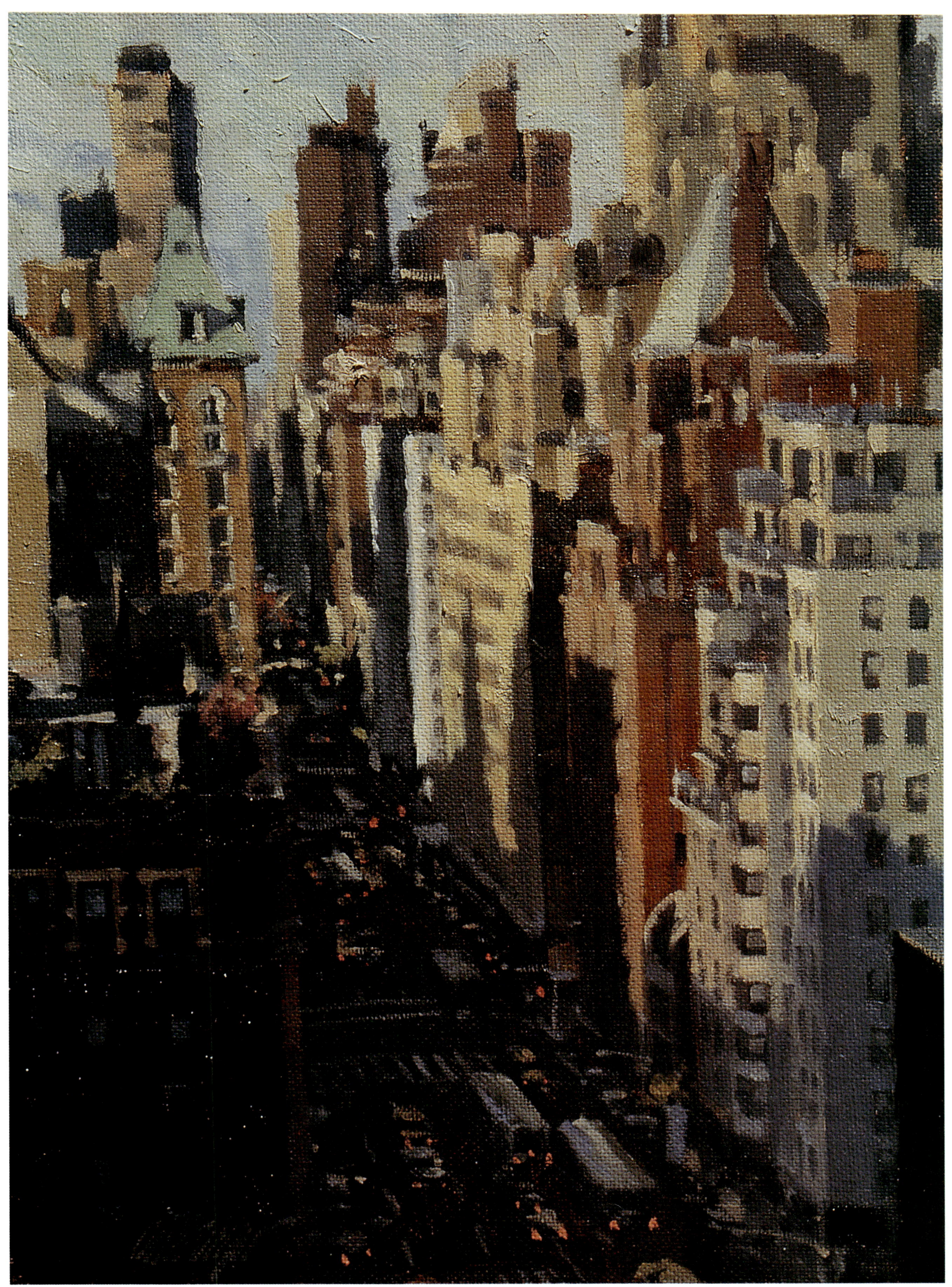

7 My heightened perspective already serves to emphasize my focal point—the long, narrow street in shadow—so it's not necessary to add too much more detail here. To finish, I apply quick dots or strokes in the areas that really stand out, such as the high-lights on the sunlit buildings, the street lights, and the tail-lights on the cars. Then, after I check to be sure I have accurate proportions and a good balance of colors and values, my painting is complete.

Using Light and Shadow

with Michael Obermeyer

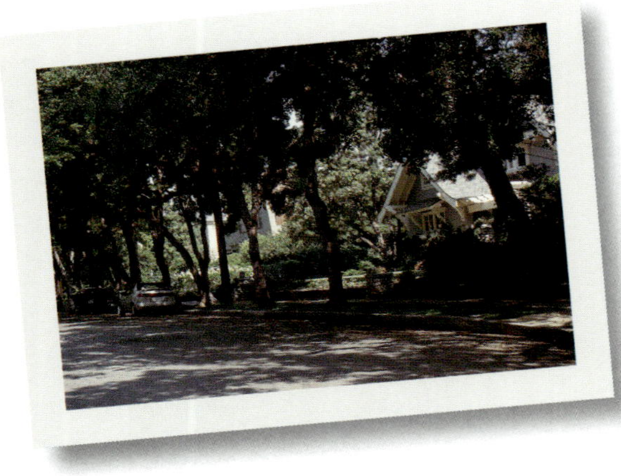

CAPTURING THE MOMENT It's not the beautiful Craftsman house that initially attracted me to this scene but the sunlit yard and shadowed street; I wanted to focus on the dynamic shapes and colors. By taking a photo, I was able to accurately record all of these details, which are constantly shifting as the sun changes position and breezes shake the trees.

The interplay between light and shadow can really pique a viewer's interest in a street scene. Incorporating subtle, natural contrasts between light and dark—such as those evident in the early morning or late afternoon—is a wonderful way to add vitality to a scene and convey a sense of the time of day. At those times, the sun is lower in the sky, creating long, cool shadows that seem to recede and warm sunlit patches that seem to "pop" forward. But nature isn't perfect—trees and rocks aren't evenly spaced—so patterns of light and shadow are a bit asymmetrical, which gives compositions a certain freshness and attracts the eye.

In this painting of a quiet street in Pasadena, California, Michael Obermeyer creates the illusion of sunlight through the effective use of color and value. In the shadows, Michael includes both a wide range of cool values and spots of reflected light, a variation that creates a sense of depth and luminosity. The shadows also counterbalance the areas of light, holding the scene together.

COLOR PALETTE

alizarin crimson, cadmium yellow deep, cadmium yellow light, cerulean blue, raw umber, titanium white, ultramarine blue, viridian green

FOREGROUND TREES
Viridian green +
alizarin crimson

MIDDLE GROUND TREES
Viridian green + alizarin crimson + ultramarine blue + white

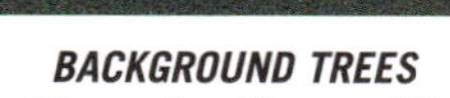

BACKGROUND TREES
Ultramarine blue + white

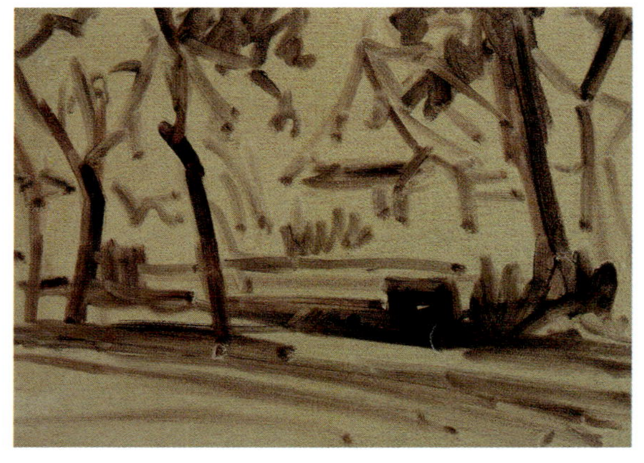

1 To begin, I "draw" the major shapes on my canvas using a thin wash of raw umber. By painting with a thin wash, I can easily make corrections to my drawing by wiping off the paint with a paper towel and re-drawing. This first step is done rather quickly, and I pay little attention to detail.

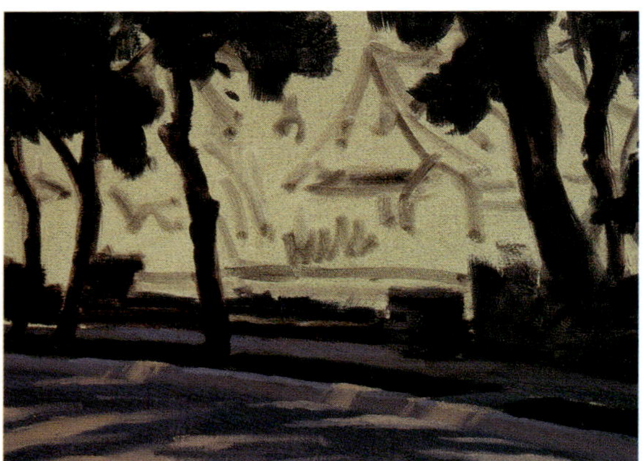

2 Next I block in the deepest values, painting the darks of the trees with a thin mix of viridian green and alizarin crimson to avoid visible brushstrokes. Using a bristle brush, which holds more paint, I begin the sun-dappled street with a thicker application of alizarin crimson, cadmium yellow light, and white.

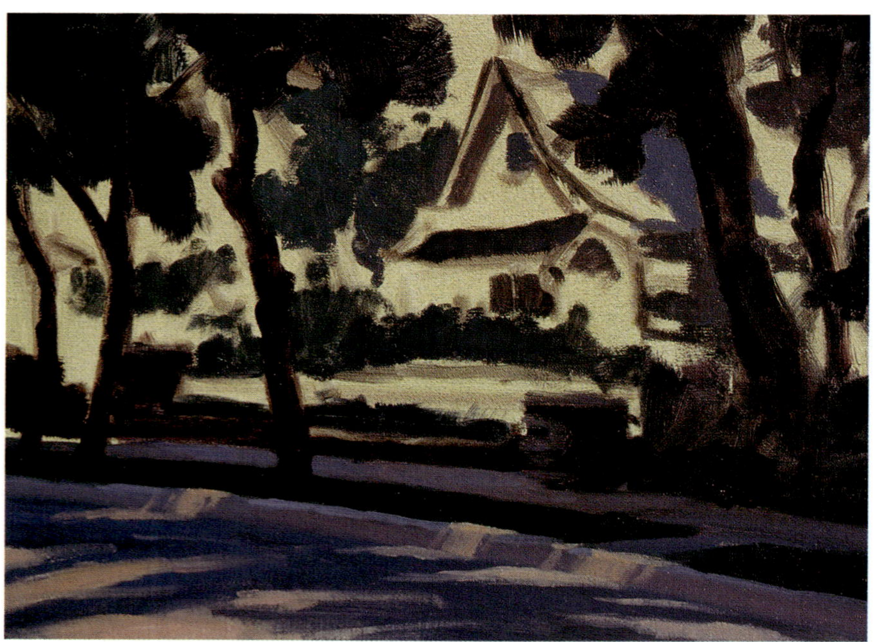

3 Next I add a little bit of ultramarine blue and titanium white to the mixture of alizarin crimson and viridian green. Then I use this mix to begin painting the background trees, which are cooler and lighter in value than the foreground colors. For the dark shapes on the house, I use alizarin crimson, ultramarine blue, and raw umber.

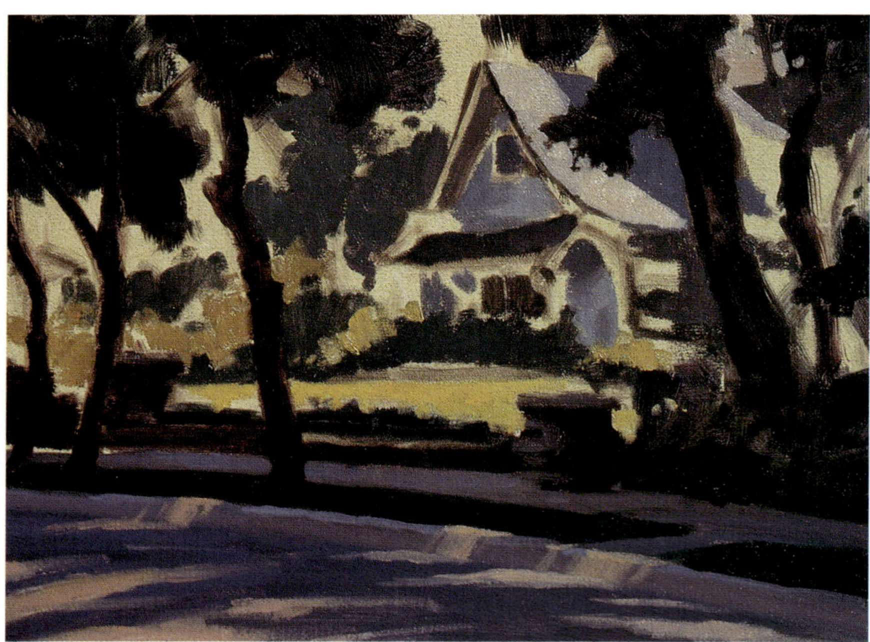

4 Now I begin painting the light colors, always keeping in mind the way the colors relate to one another. At this stage, I concentrate on developing color blocks rather than specific shapes. I subtly vary the color in the different light and shadow areas to create mood and feeling.

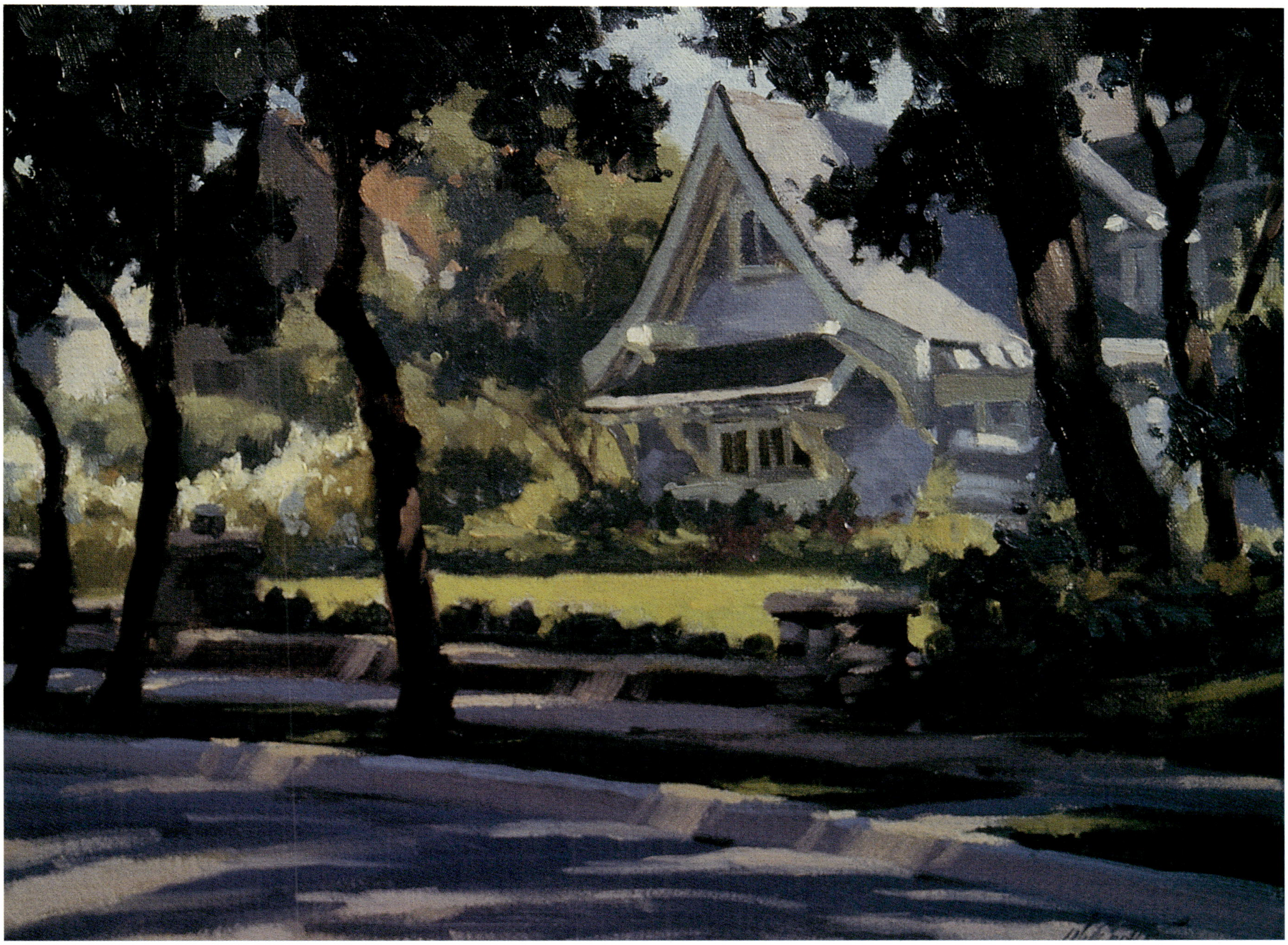

7 In my final step, while continuing to add details, I "push" my values, placing the lightest highlights on the eaves of the house, the sun-dappled road, and the field of flowers. I also adjust the edges where necessary, making them softer on background elements and harder on the foreground trees. Then I punch up the darks in the shadow of the trees and shrubbery, but I avoid adding too much detail on the house, instead keeping the shapes simple and loose.

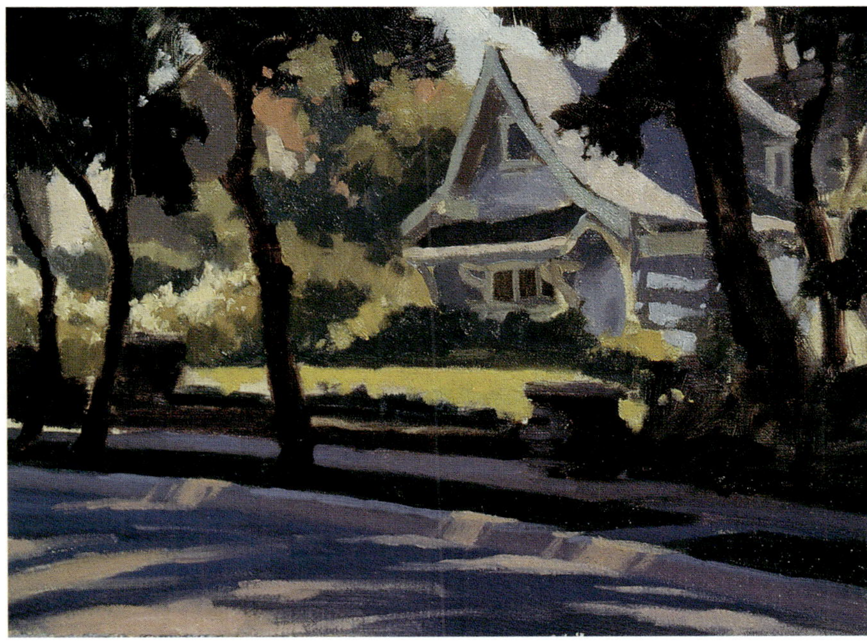

5 Next I paint the sky using cerulean blue mixed with cadmium yellow light and generous amounts of titanium white. For the sunlit lawn, I create a mixture of viridian green, cadmium yellow light, and a bit of both cadmium yellow deep and white. I work throughout the composition, often stepping back to check my values and color.

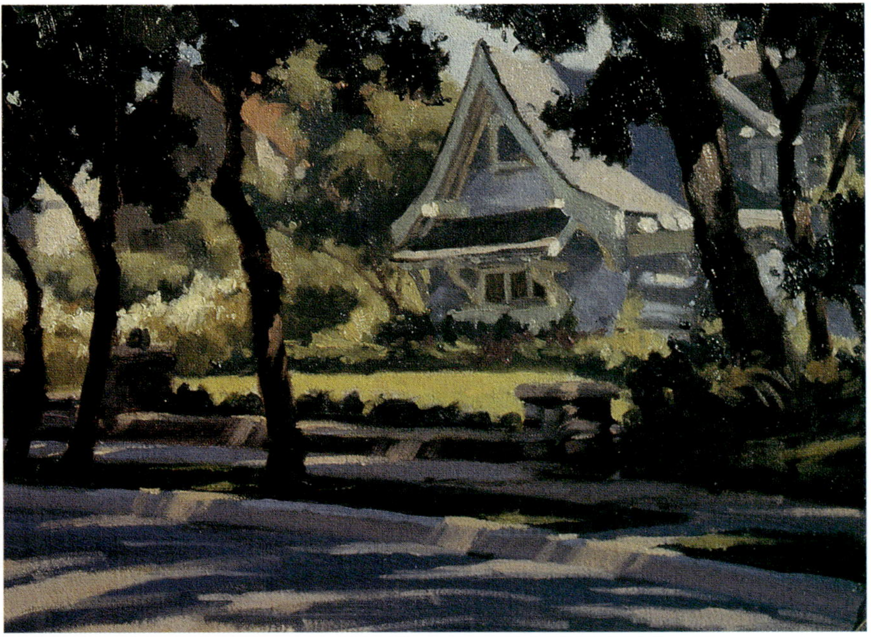

6 Using small flat and bright brushes, I paint the smaller shapes and details, such as the window edges and flowers, as well as some architectural details and the shapes of the foliage in the foreground trees. I balance the dark tree trunks in the right foreground of the painting with the bright highlight of the flowers on the left.

CREATING ATMOSPHERIC PERSPECTIVE

WITH MICHAEL OBERMEYER

When painting street scenes, the use of atmospheric perspective is critical. Outdoors the impurities in the air (such as moisture and dust) block out some sunlight, so objects in the distance appear less distinct and with softer edges than do those in the foreground. And because the longer, red wavelengths of light are filtered out, objects in the distance also appear cooler and bluer. In this painting, Michael Obermeyer employs *atmospheric perspective*, saving the brightest colors for the nearest elements. He paints objects farther away with less detail and muted, cool colors, and he applies the most detail to the foreground of the scene.

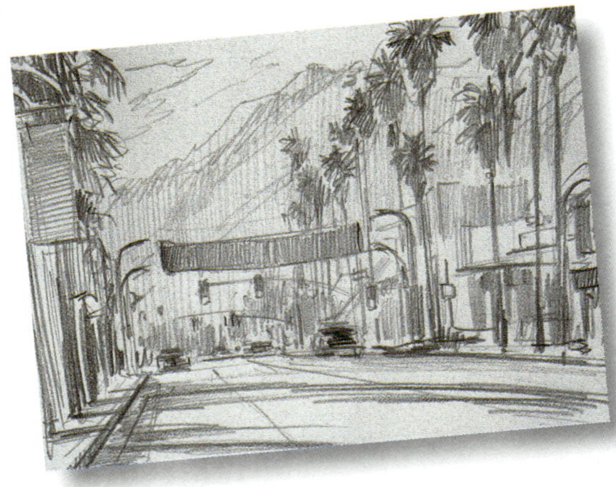

CREATING A VALUE SKETCH This southern California street makes a busy composition, so first I work out the values in a pencil sketch of the scene. Here I outline how I'll use atmospheric perspective in my painting; for example, note the way the distant mountains are penciled in more lightly than the foreground elements are.

COLOR PALETTE

alizarin crimson, cadmium yellow deep, cadmium yellow medium, raw umber, titanium white, ultramarine blue, viridian green

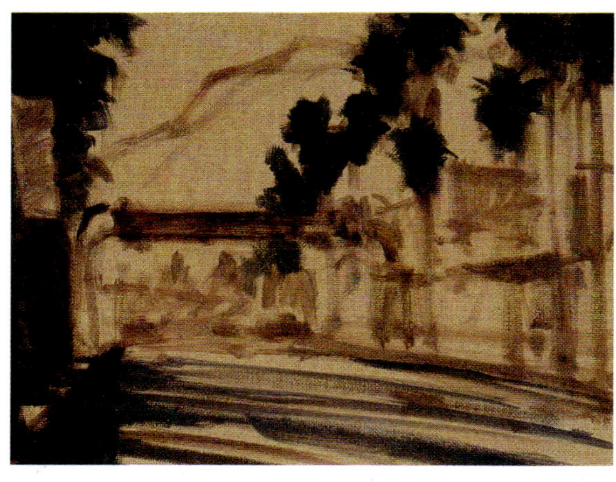

1 When I'm satisfied with my initial sketch, I begin loosely "drawing" on the canvas with a medium sable brush and a thin wash of raw umber. (With the thin wash, I can easily make corrections by wiping off the paint with a paper towel.) I also block in the darkest shapes using a mix of viridian green, ultramarine blue, and alizarin crimson.

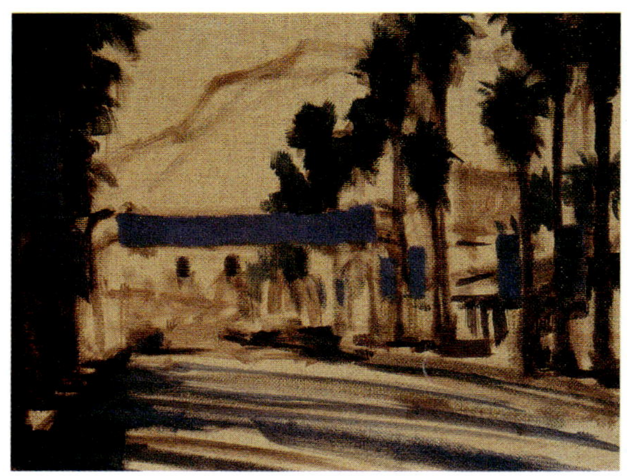

2 Now I continue to develop the dark values, adding more shadows on the street with a purplish-gray mix of ultramarine blue and alizarin crimson. For unity, I use this same mixture to add the hanging street banner, keeping the value of the banner similar to that of the trees to maintain a sense of balance in the painting.

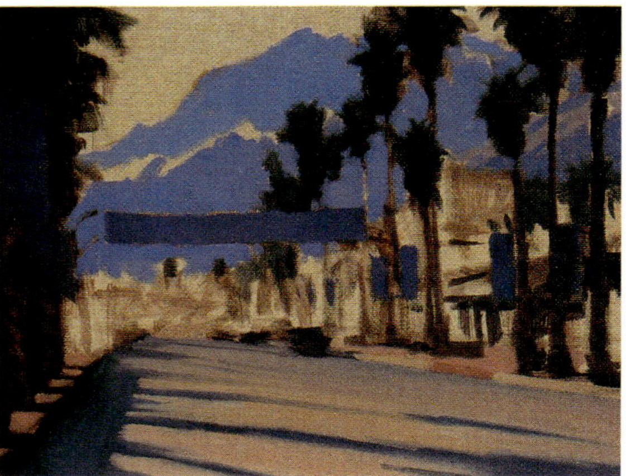

3 Next I finish blocking in my darkest shapes, still using a thin mix of paint and medium flat sable brushes. My earlier sketch allows me to paint with confidence, since I have charted a path for my composition already. I fill in the mountains with a lighter ultramarine blue; the soft, cool color helps suggest their distance.

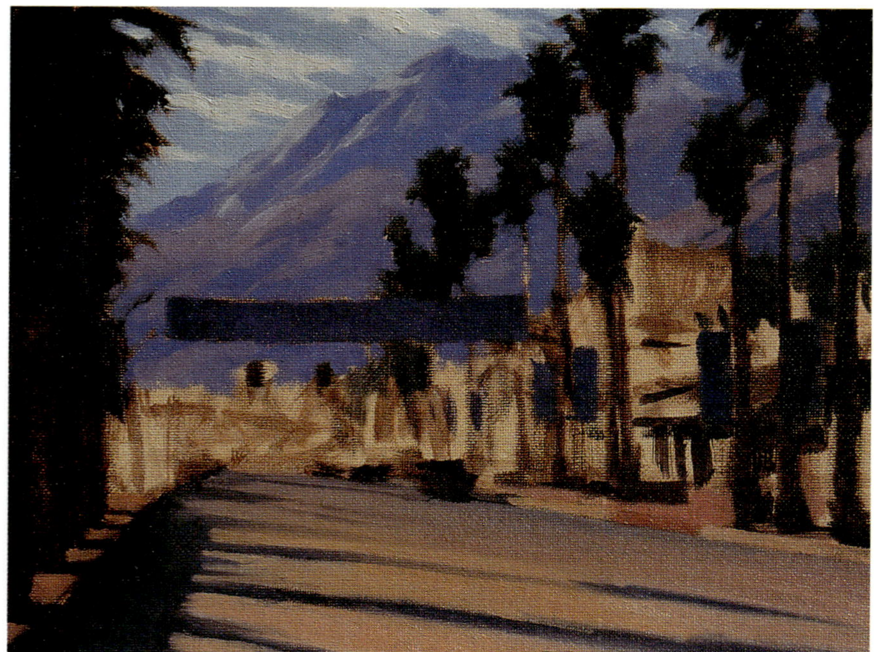

4 I switch to a flat bristle brush to paint the street, using a thicker application of cadmium yellow deep mixed with alizarin crimson and titanium white. I keep the edges of the shadows in the street soft, avoiding too much detail in this foreground area since it is not the focus of the scene. I use the same color mixture to fully block in the mountains in the background and some of the dark building shapes. I adjust the mixture to make it both lighter and cooler as I work into the distance.

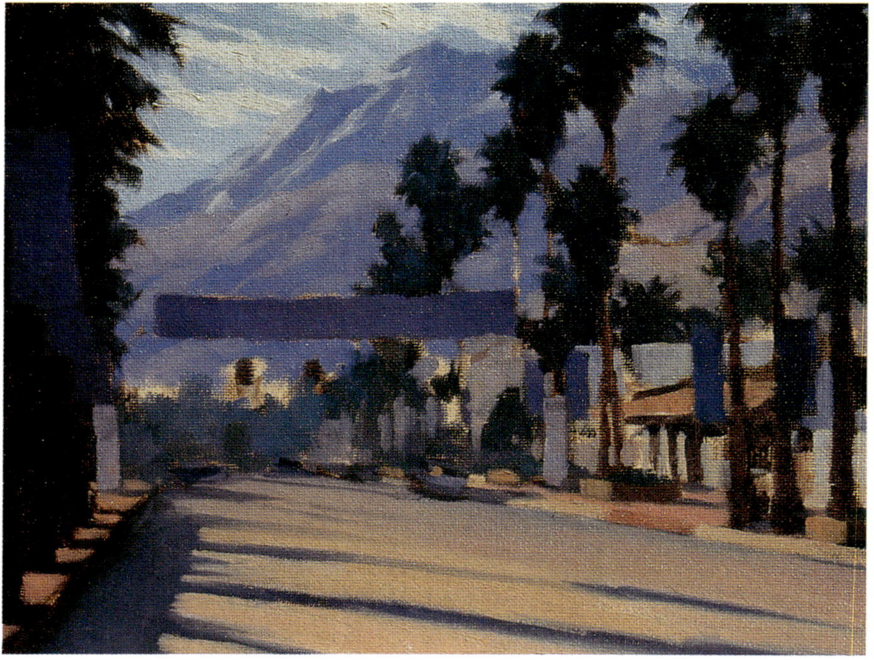

5 I lighten cerulean blue with titanium white and apply this color to the light areas of the mountains as well as the sky. My middle values are important because they serve as a bridge between the dark shadows and trees of the foreground and the light blues and grays of the mountains and sky in the distance. I constantly adjust the values as I work, maintaining a balance by considering all the values and colors of the painting.

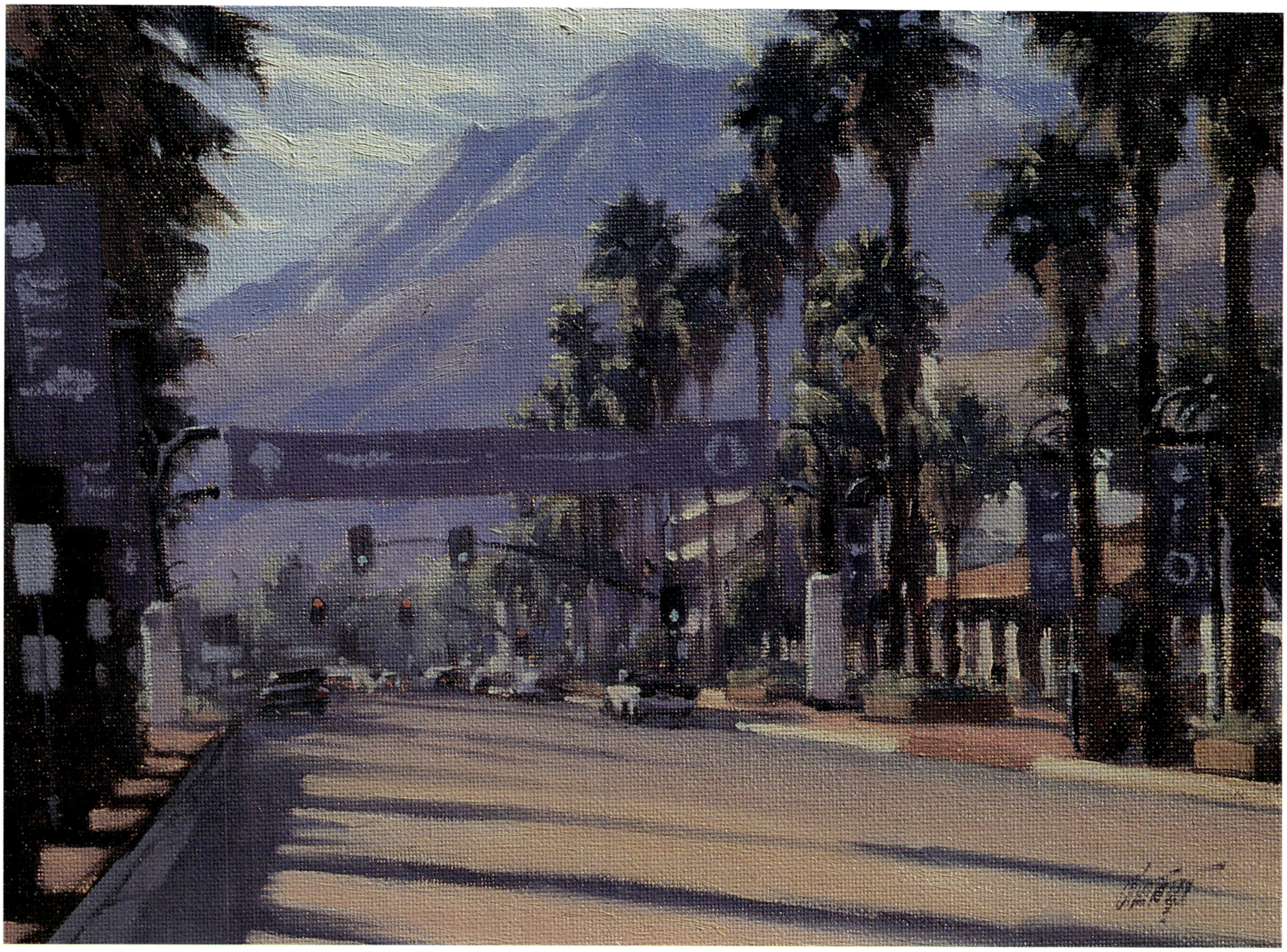

8 For the final touches, first I add a few highlights to the palm trees using a mix of viridian green, cadmium yellow deep, cadmium yellow medium, and titanium white. Next I add a few additional highlights and touch up details throughout the painting. Now I step back to assess the painting as a whole, and I adjust the edges and values as needed until I am satisfied with all the shapes and colors. Then my painting of an early morning in *Palm Canyon* is complete.

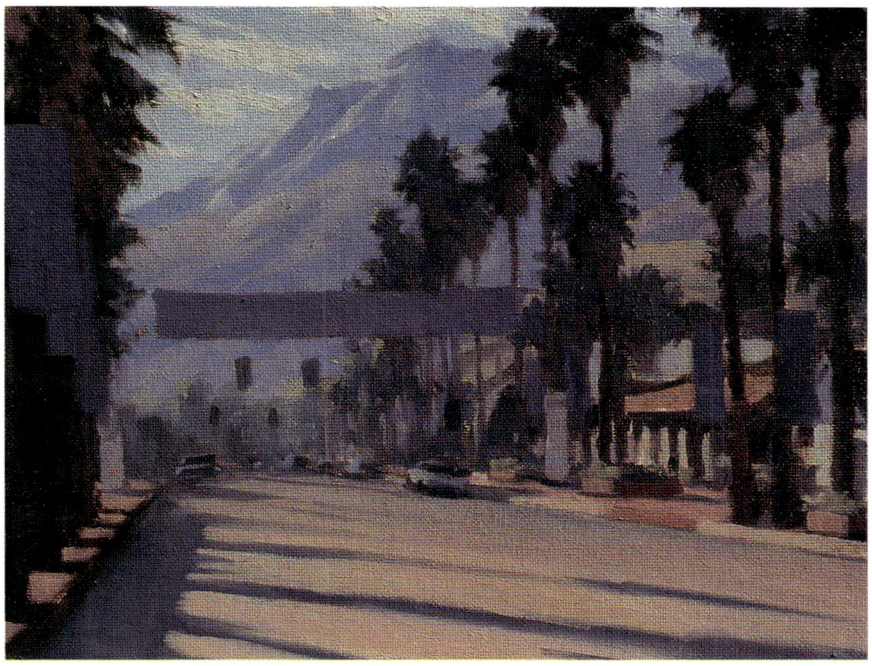

6 Next I begin blocking in the smaller shapes of the background trees and the buildings, again using thick paint applied with small flat bristle brushes. I use thin washes of paint and smaller sable brushes to block in smaller dark shapes, including shadows and cars. With a complex subject like this, a good drawing and correct perspective are as important as the right colors and values, so I make any necessary adjustments to my drawing as I work.

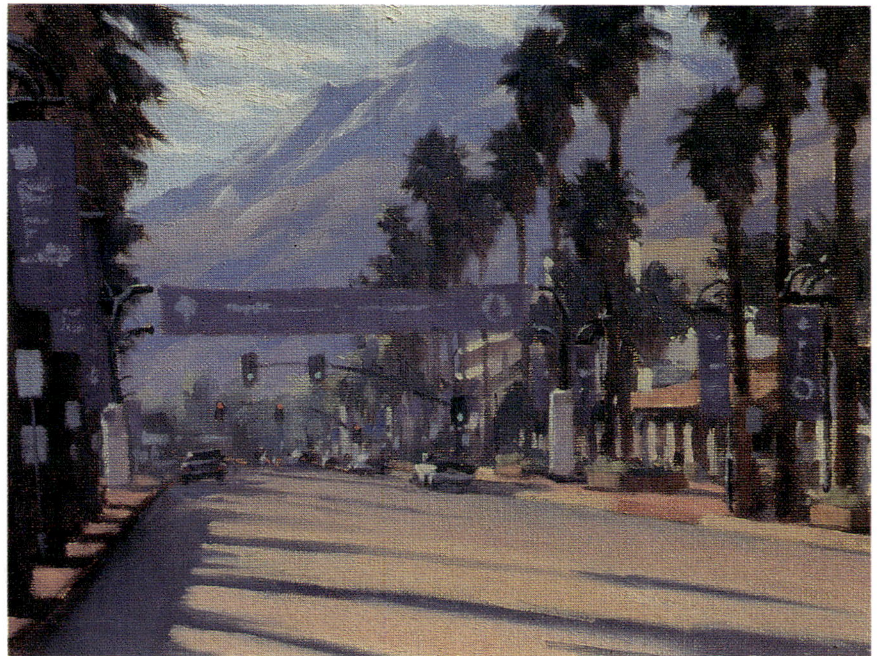

7 Now I use small, flat bristle brushes to block in the smaller shapes of buildings with cerulean blue and a lot of titanium white. I add a touch of cadmium yellow light to the mixture for the lighter areas of the cars and details on the street, sidewalks, lamp posts, and tree trunks. Again, I use thicker paint for the lighter areas and thinner applications for the darks. With my smallest sable brush, I pick up alizarin crimson, viridian green, and titanium white to add detail to the stop lights and street signs.

Emphasizing a Focal Point

with Caroline Zimmermann

A painting that highlights the architectural detail of a building is a great addition to any portfolio. It is excellent practice to stand in the midst of an overstimulating environment—noisy traffic, a lot of signs, bustling crowds—and seek out a lone subject of beauty that captures your interest. Selecting a narrow focus for a painting eliminates the distractions, leaving only the object of interest. Zooming in on a tight focal point, such as a doorway or a window, immediately creates a memorable street scene.

In the Tuscan countryside, where Caroline Zimmermann discovered the subject for this painting, doors are often as individual as people are. And this closeup view allows Caroline to focus on all the features of this doorway, from the texture of the building materials to the variety of potted plants and flowers—elements that would have been lost in the noise of a more broadly focused, chaotic scene.

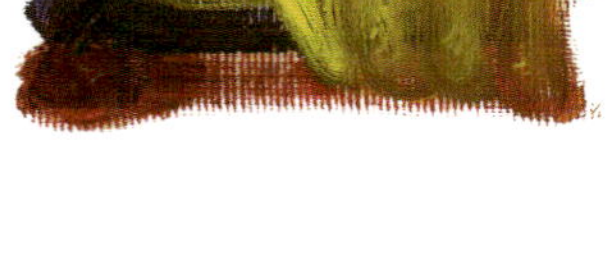

TAKING NOTES Photographs are reliable for capturing the overall impression of a scene, but not everything you see can be captured on film. Taking a notebook along on your travels in addition to your camera allows you to record quick impressions of the textures and colors you see.

COLOR PALETTE

alizarin crimson, cadmium red light, cadmium yellow light, cadmium yellow medium, dioxazine purple, Indian yellow, lemon yellow, rose madder, sap green, transparent orange, ultramarine blue

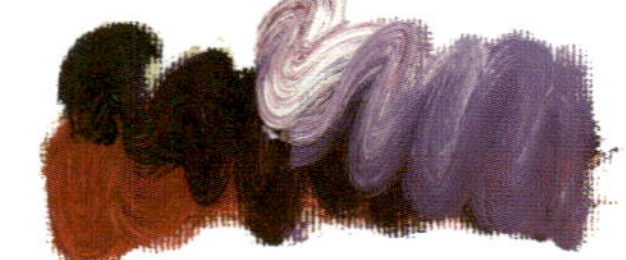

DOOR
*Alizarin crimson +
dioxazine purple +
cadmium yellow medium*

STAIRS/CEMENT
*Alizarin crimson +
dioxazine purple +
titanium white*

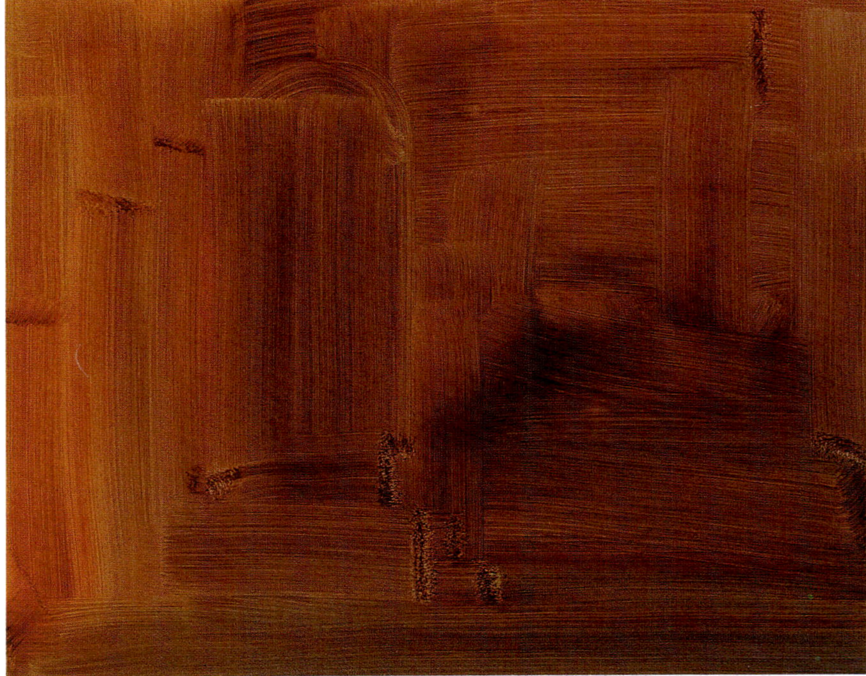

1 Using a large chip brush, I begin an underpainting with colors that will subtly radiate warmth through the subsequent layers of paint, ultimately creating a more vibrant image. First I thin each color with odorless mineral solvent to create fluid, transparent pigments; then I completely cover the canvas with a transparent wash of Indian yellow, transparent orange, and dioxazine purple, using broad strokes that sweep in the direction of the elements and eliminating the white of the canvas entirely. Next I set aside the canvas, giving the fumes of the solvent a chance to evaporate.

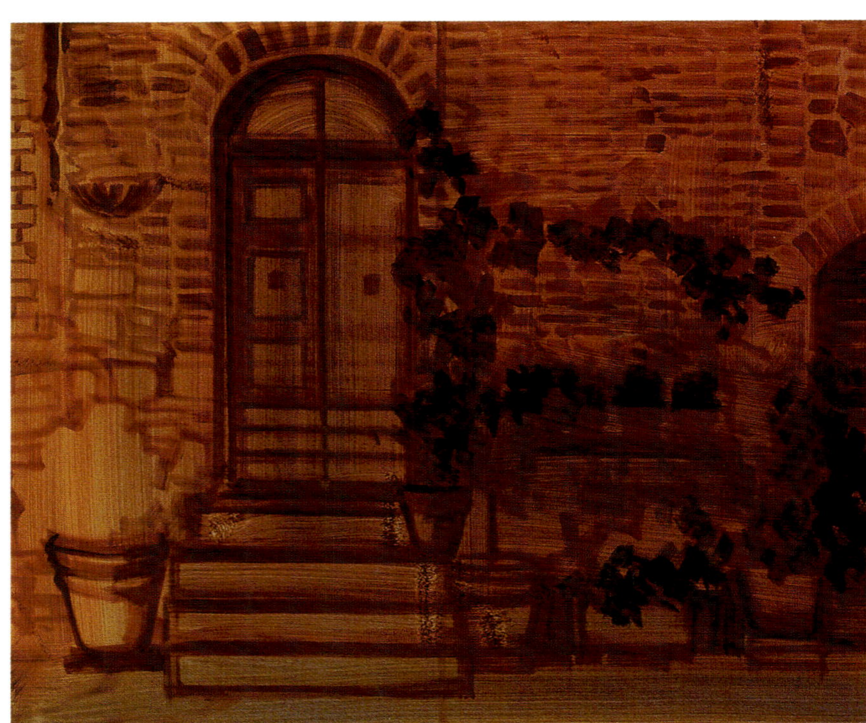

2 I liquefy my sketching paint (dioxazine purple mixed with alizarin crimson) with solvent until it's the consistency of heavy cream, and then I begin to establish my dark areas. Using a flat brush, I loosely draw the door and the pots. I also establish a few other shapes and patterns, blocking in the somewhat irregular pattern of the hand-laid bricks.

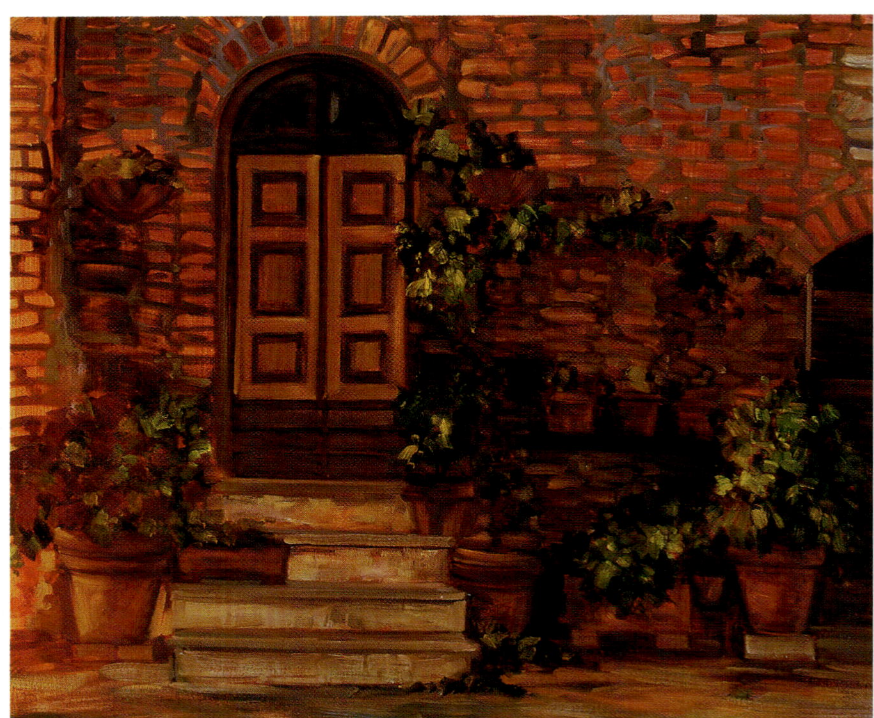

3 Now I define the door with a base mix of alizarin crimson and dioxazine purple. For the stairs and cement, I add white to the base, mixing in a touch of cadmium yellow on the street and stairs. For the wood panel, I add cadmium yellow medium. For the foliage, I use the base with sap green, adding cadmium yellow light for lighter layers. The flowers are pure alizarin crimson.

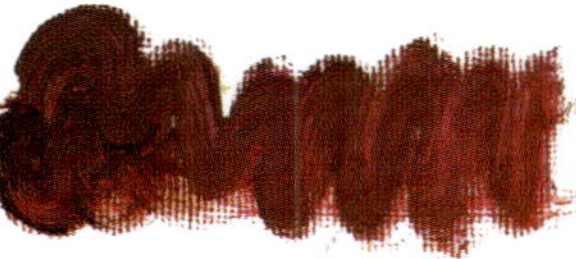

DARK HYDRANGEA
Alizarin crimson + magenta

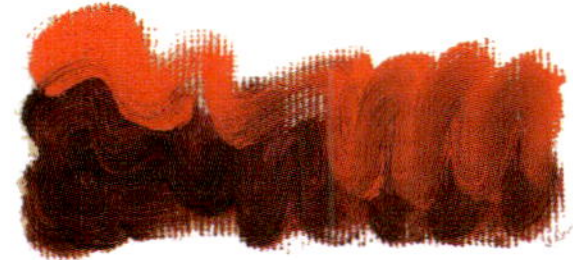

MEDIUM HYDRANGEA
*Alizarin crimson + magenta
+ cadmium red medium*

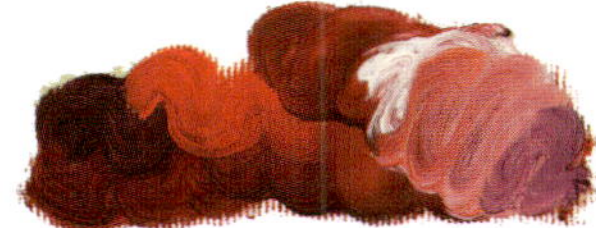

LIGHT HYDRANGEA
*Alizarin crimson + magenta
+ cadmium red light + rose
madder + titanium white*

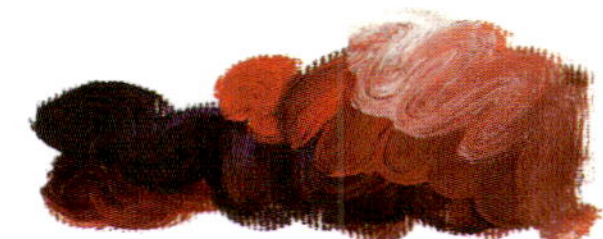

BRICKS AND POTS
*Alizarin crimson + dioxazine
purple + cadmium red
medium + titanium white*

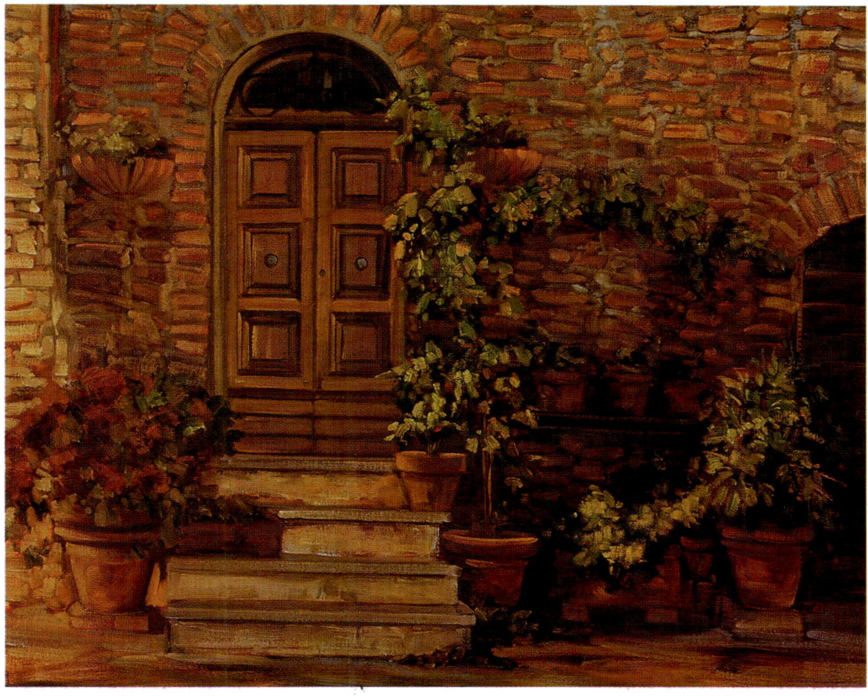

4 To bring out a golden glow in the door, I add cadmium yellow medium to the alizarin crimson and dioxazine purple mix. I add more cadmium yellow light to the foliage mix to bring out a shimmer. Then, to further define the bricks and terra cotta planters, I take the alizarin crimson and dioxazine purple mix and add cadmium red first, then cadmium red light. I vary the bricks and pots by adding a touch of cadmium yellow light; the addition of a touch of titanium white provides texture. I also add a bit of magenta to alizarin crimson to add variation to the flowers; I mix in an additional touch of cadmium red light to create the flowers' form.

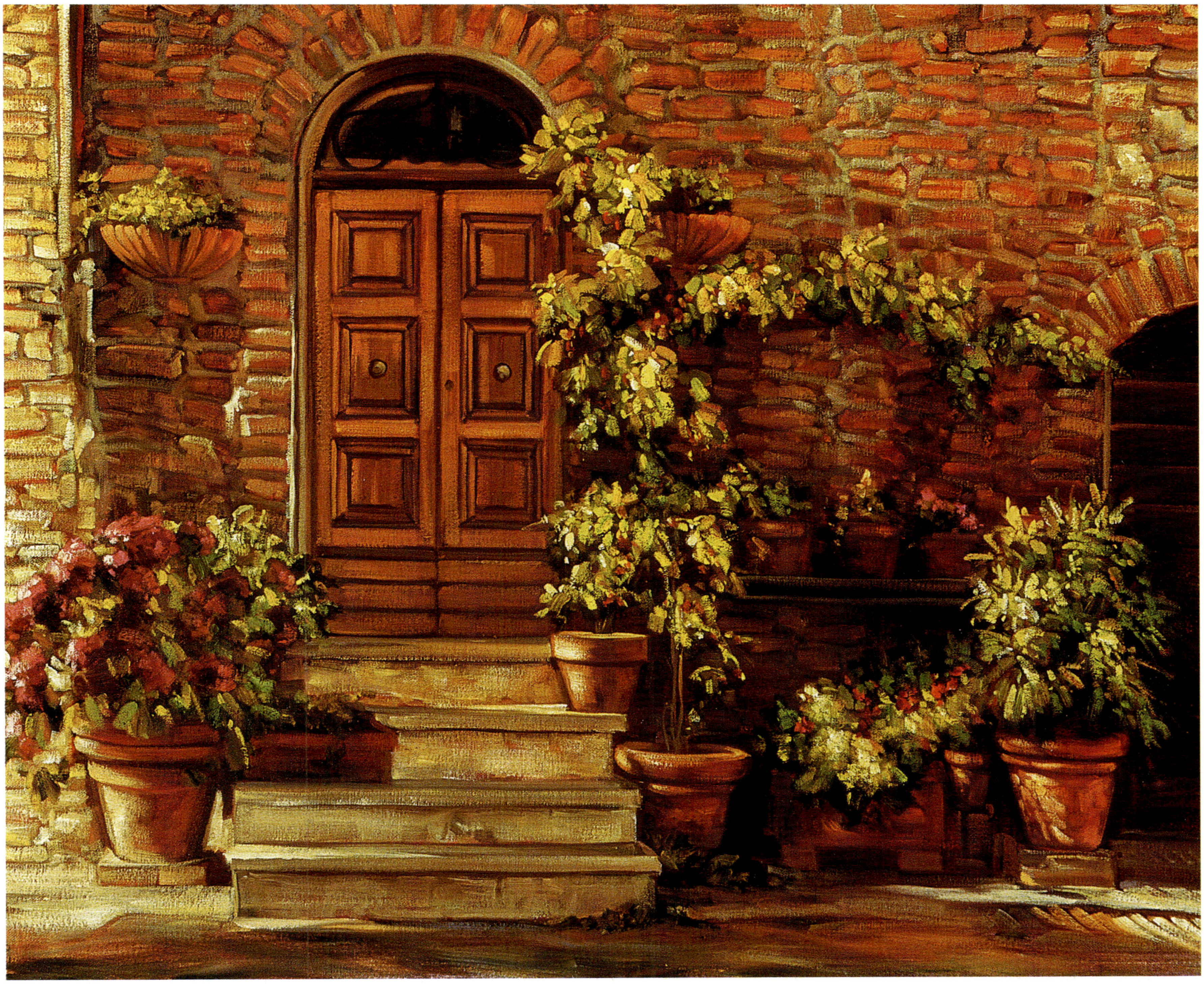

5 Because I usually work from dark to light, I've saved the highlights for last or, as I like to call it, the "icing on the cake" step. First I mix titanium white with small amounts of cadmium yellow light to highlight the bricks, the terra cotta pots, the street, and the stairs. I add a touch of sap green to this mixture for the foliage highlights. Then, to add a splash of color, I highlight the flowers with a mixture of cadmium red, rose madder, and white, sometimes adding more yellow or red for variety. I try to see the shapes of the lightest lights as I apply the paint in a spontaneous, direct manner with a small flat brush; these tiny touches make all the difference.

DEVELOPING BOLD COLORS

WITH CAROLINE ZIMMERMANN

Much of the joy of painting street scenes comes from the pleasure of turning a simple locale into an extraordinary painting. But the muted tones of natural brick or stone may leave you aching for a more colorful composition. What at first may appear to be a dull, earthen brick building can easily be enlivened by using bold colors. Look beyond a neutral palette of grays, browns, and beiges and punch up the scene with stronger accent colors.

Caroline Zimmermann was attracted to bright, warm colors in this walkway in Venice in spring, which reflect the textures and hues of everyday life in this picturesque Italian town. Here she uses deep reds, yellows, and purples to bring life and interest to the old and weathered structures without overpowering the character of the architecture. She also reserves her boldest colors for the sunlit walls and pathway, which frame the figures and help to unify all the elements. Try experimenting with the rich, deep colors of her palette to see how you can add strength and vitality to your own paintings of street scenes, whatever the location.

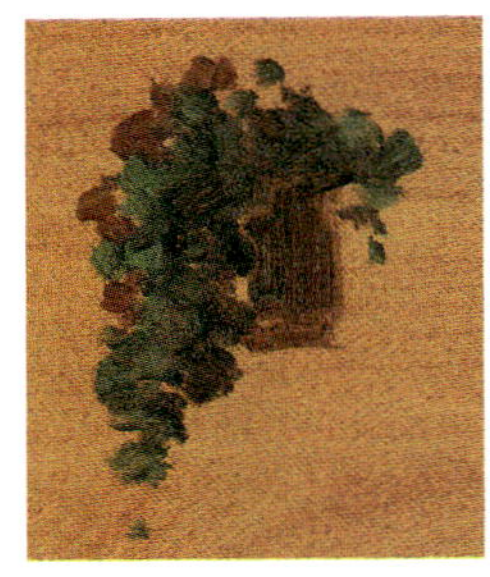
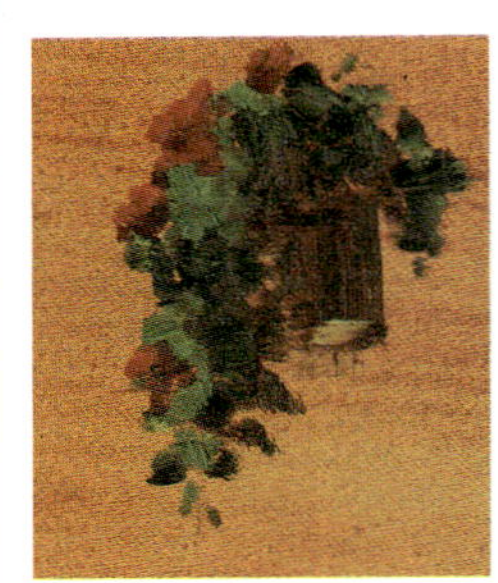
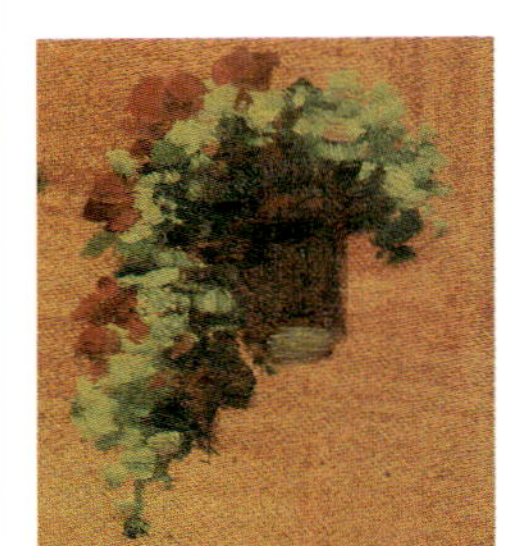

The baskets of hydrangea flowers that line the windows of this quaint street provide unity to the scene. The bold red flowers harmonize with the warm yellows and pinks of the buildings. And even the greens take on a bold, bright tone because of the warm underpainting's influence. To develop the baskets, I layer in the darkest values first, swiping in the basket and the dark foliage values, followed by cadmium red medium for the flowers. Next I paint the foliage mid-tones, applying cadmium red medium mixed with alizarin crimson to the flowers. Then I finish with the lightest values of the foliage and touches of alizarin crimson highlights on the buds.

COLOR PALETTE

alizarin crimson, cadmium red medium, cadmium yellow medium, dioxazine purple, Indian yellow, lemon yellow, phthalo blue, sap green, titanium white, transparent orange, ultramarine blue

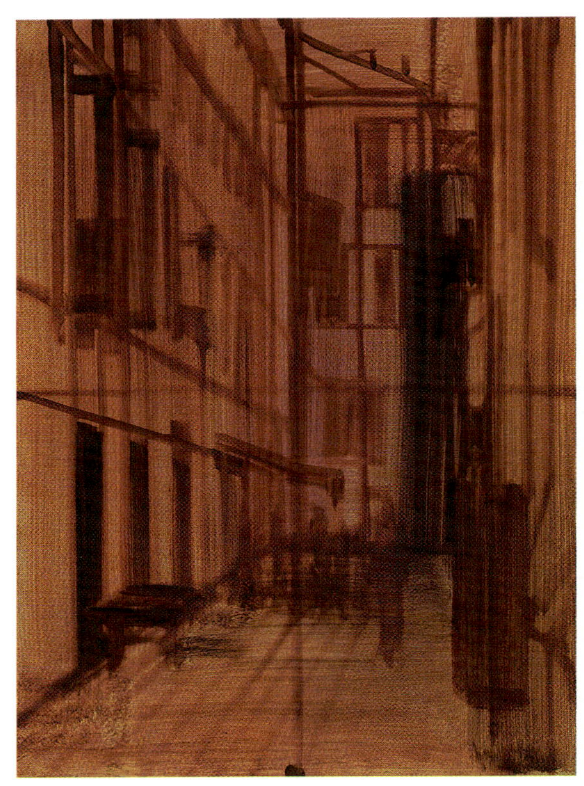

1 For my underpainting, I apply a mixture of alizarin crimson, Indian yellow, and transparent orange, thinned with solvent. Then I loosely sketch on top of the undercolor with a thinned mix of alizarin crimson and dioxazine purple. When working on architectural compositions, my first marks with the brush onto the color-washed canvas are lightly drawn perpendicular lines, which indicate the mid-points of each side. These marks establish the foundations of the composition. Next I loosely draw perspective lines with my brush, following the general movement of the composition. I keep my definition to a minimum so that I still have the liberty to change my mind about the placement of some of the elements of the composition later.

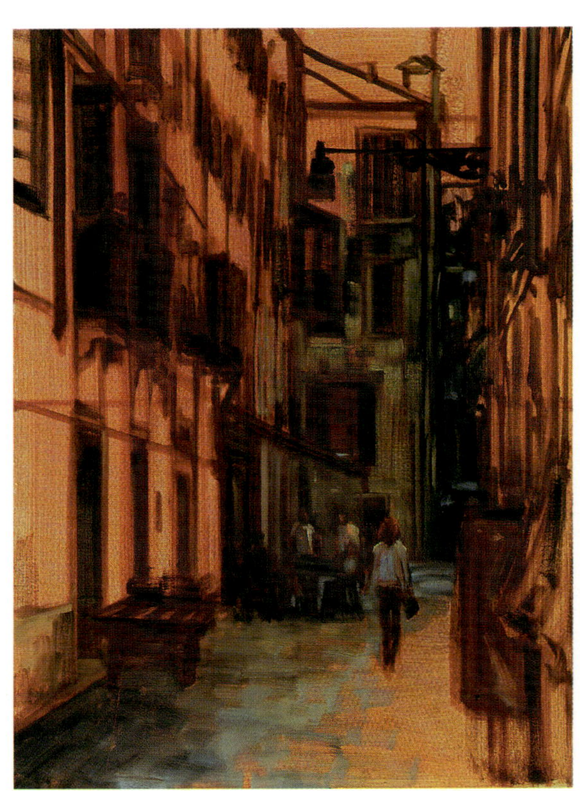

2 With a medium flat brush and the liquefied alizarin and dioxazine purple, I plot out the dark areas of the street, the figures, and the structures, noting the general direction of the light source and observing its effects on the shapes and placement of the shadows. Using a smaller flat brush, I address the windows and dark alley with a mix of dioxazine purple, alizarin crimson, and ultramarine blue. (I mix a large batch of this color, as it will become the base for the medium tones in step three.) I add sap green to the mix to create the dark green of the shutters, the window box foliage, and the cart in the foreground. Then I add a touch of titanium white to the darks to establish the shirts of the figures as well as the lighter areas of shadow in the street.

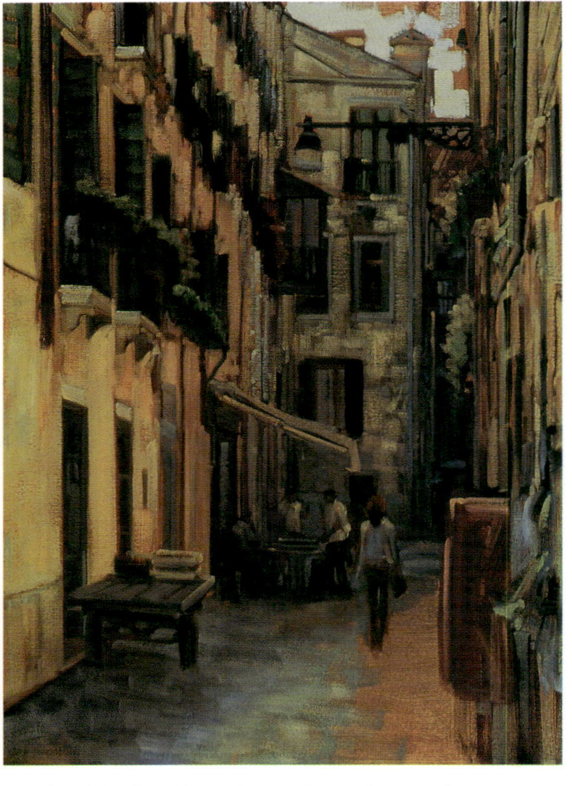

3 Now I begin to layer the medium values on the street, adding more titanium white to the dark tones from step two. I add small amounts of cadmium yellow medium to the mix for the buildings, varying the yellow shades by touching in alizarin crimson for the pink and peach colors. As I paint, I consciously allow the underpainting to reveal itself to create the texture of aged stucco. For the medium tones of the foliage, I add sap green and cadmium yellow light to the base mix. And for the classic Italian mailbox on the right, I add cadmium red medium and alizarin crimson to create the mid-tones. With the same color, I dot on the geraniums in the window boxes. To begin the highlights, I mix titanium white and a spot of phthalo blue and block in the sky.

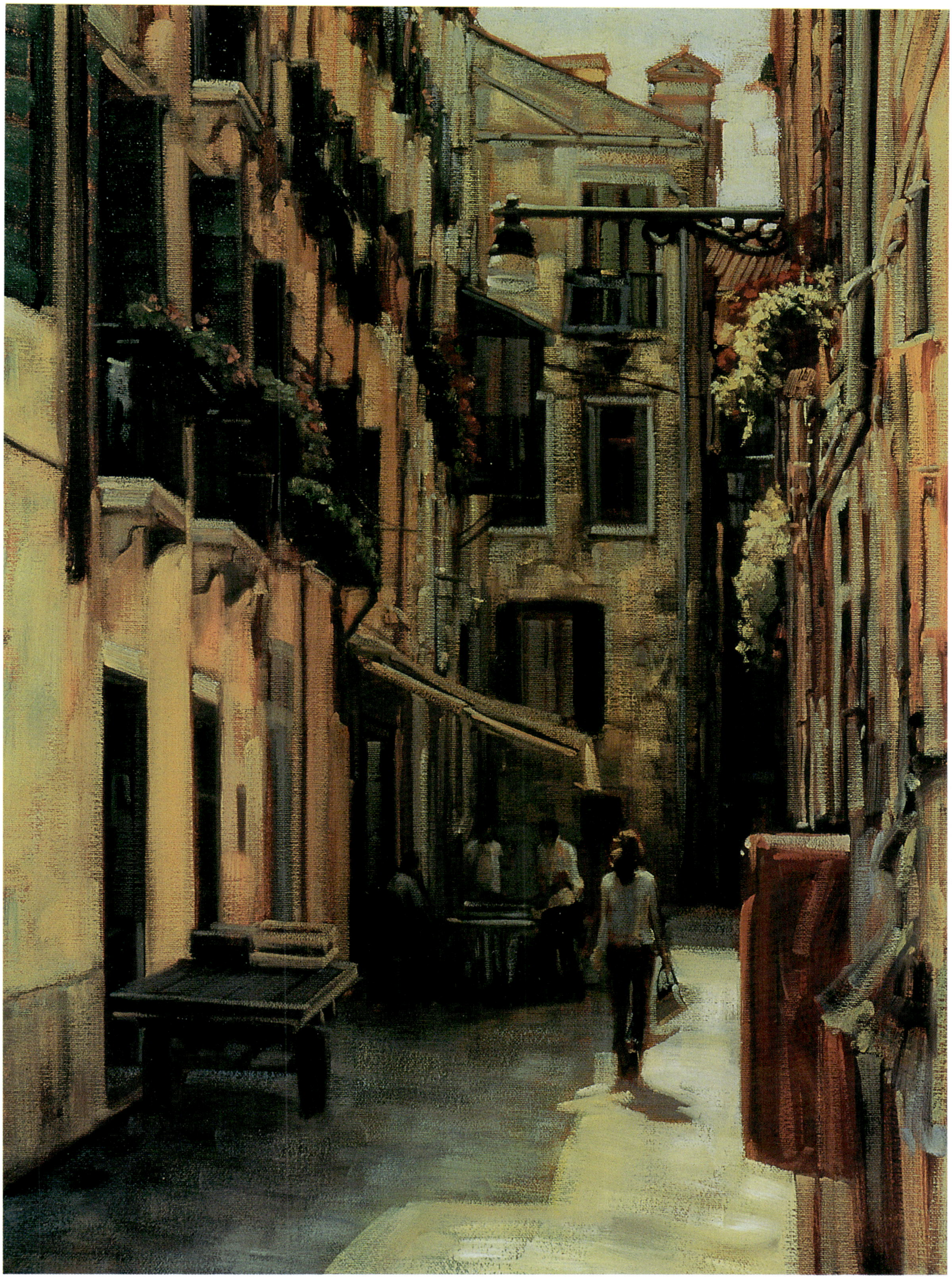

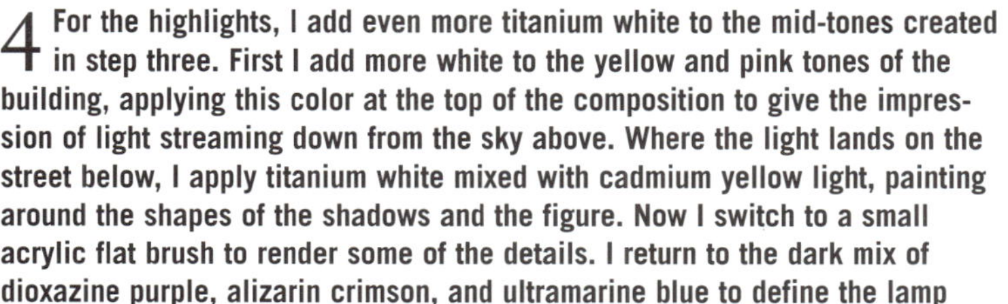

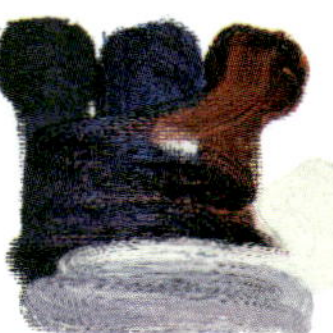

**STREETS AND
SHADOWS**
*Dioxazine purple
+ ultramarine blue
+ alizarin crimson
(+ white for
highlights)*

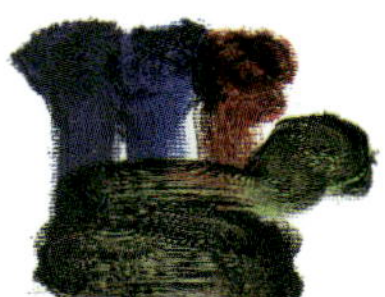

**DARK WINDOW
BOX FOLIAGE**
*Dioxazine purple +
ultramarine blue +
alizarin crimson +
sap green*

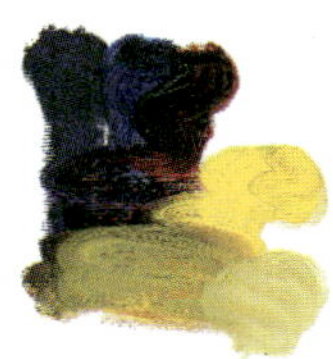

**WALL COLOR
(YELLOWS)**
*Dioxazine purple +
ultramarine blue +
alizarin crimson +
white + cadmium
yellow light*

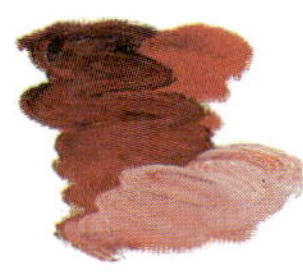

MAILBOX
*Alizarin crimson +
cadmium red
medium + white*

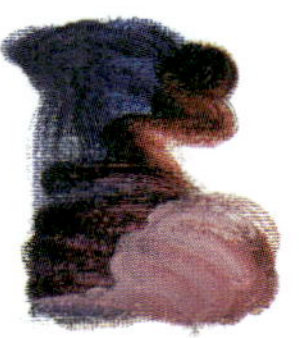

WALL COLOR (PINKS)
*Dioxazine purple +
ultramarine blue +
alizarin crimson +
titanium white*

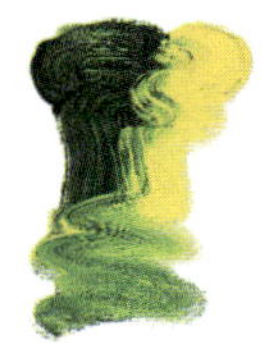

**MEDIUM WINDOW
BOX FOLIAGE**
*Sap green +
cadmium yellow
light*

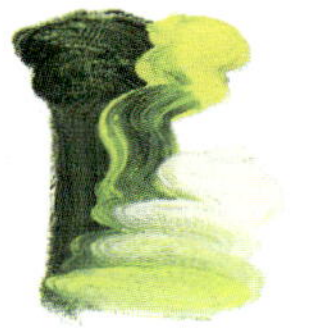

**LIGHT WINDOW BOX
FOLIAGE**
*Sap green + lemon
yellow + titanium
white*

4 For the highlights, I add even more titanium white to the mid-tones created in step three. First I add more white to the yellow and pink tones of the building, applying this color at the top of the composition to give the impression of light streaming down from the sky above. Where the light lands on the street below, I apply titanium white mixed with cadmium yellow light, painting around the shapes of the shadows and the figure. Now I switch to a small acrylic flat brush to render some of the details. I return to the dark mix of dioxazine purple, alizarin crimson, and ultramarine blue to define the lamp post, streaking on some of this color with the edge of the brush to give the appearance of wires. Next I pick up the titanium white and cadmium yellow light mixture to highlight the lamp, the tops of the shutters, and the pipes. Sap green, lemon yellow, and titanium white create the highlight color on the leaves in the window boxes. And cadmium red light with a touch of white highlights the sunlit geraniums and the mailbox in the foreground. I save the pure white for the finishing touches, adding highlights to the crisp shoulder of the woman's shirt and the glass of the lampshade.

SIMPLIFYING A SUBJECT

WITH CAROLINE ZIMMERMANN

Certain street scenes provide heartier challenges for the painters, especially those laden with details. A street swarming with cars, a boardwalk crowded with people, or a market filled with flowers are all visually enticing. And, despite the large number of details and the variety of colors and textures, these busy scenes shouldn't intimidate you. It's possible to capture the impression of the scene without rendering every form exactly. By planning the details and including only what is essential, you can simplify the scene to a manageable level.

Caroline Zimmermann was immediately attracted to this springtime portrait of a morning flower market located in Provence, France. To simplify the composition—which includes more than a thousand subjects—Caroline searched for repeating patterns and colors in the scene. By focusing on these broader elements and rendering only just enough detail to suggest the subjects, she can easily depict this busy and richly colored street scene.

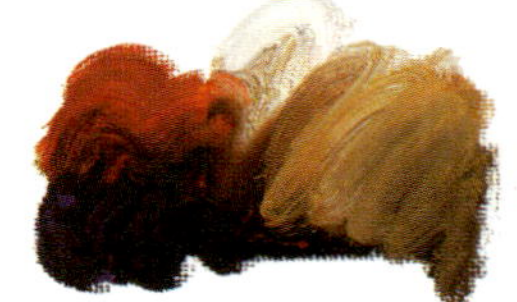

WALLS OF BUILDING
Dioxazine purple + transparent orange + titanium white

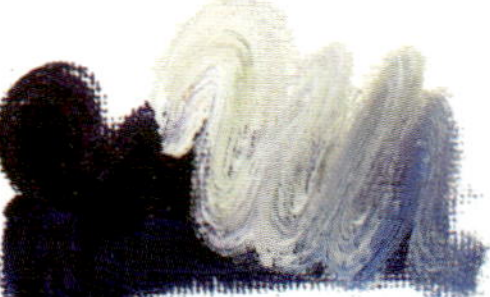

STREET AND SHADOWS
Ultramarine blue + dioxazine purple + titanium white

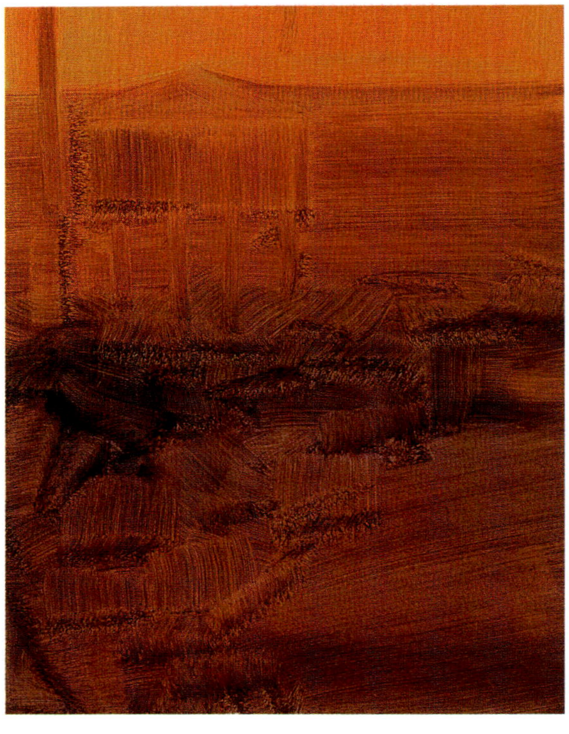

1 First I eliminate the white of the canvas, applying a thinned mixture of alizarin crimson, Indian yellow, and transparent orange with a large chip brush. I apply the paint loosely, but my brushstrokes follow the lines of the composition. Next, to establish what will later become the dark areas of the foreground, I introduce dioxazine purple to the lower part of the canvas.

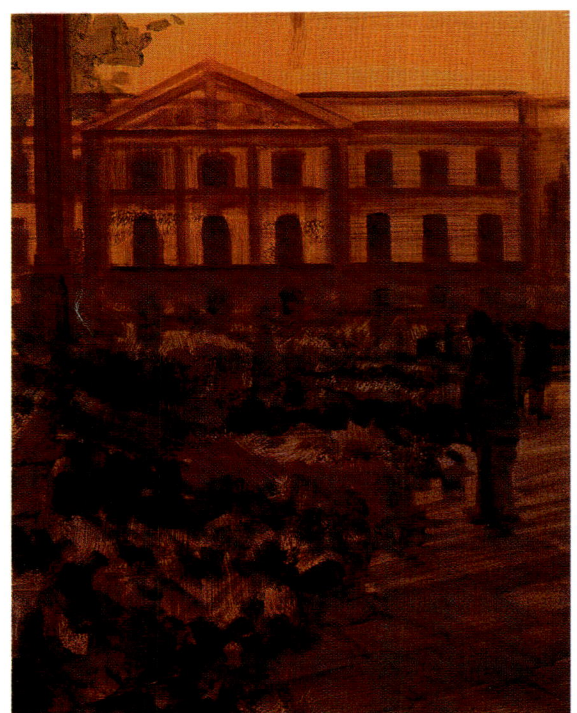

2 Now I switch to a medium bright brush to loosely indicate the patterns of the building and the mass of flowers; I use a mix of alizarin crimson and dioxazine purple that has been liquefied with solvent, making it the consistency of heavy cream. When these basic shapes are in place, I use dioxazine purple to designate the position of the flower arrangements and the main figure.

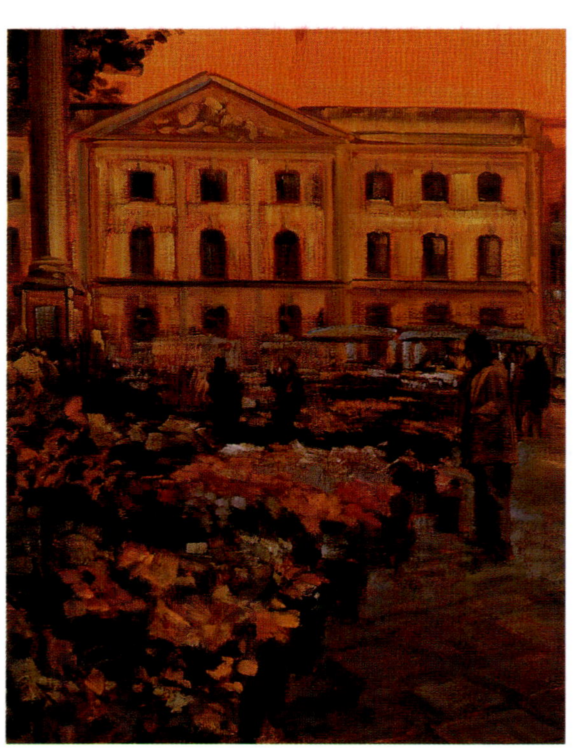

3 With a medium flat brush, I apply the deep tones of the foreground shadows, the background umbrellas, and the white flowers with a mix of ultramarine blue, titanium white, and a touch of dioxazine purple. I establish other darks within the flower arrangements using variations of dioxazine purple mixed with ultramarine blue. To this, I add cadmium yellow medium for the figure's jacket and the sunflowers, and I add sap green for the darks of the foliage. Then I move on to the building, applying a transparent orange and titanium white mix. I vary this mix with dioxazine purple to create the appearance of the travertine stone.

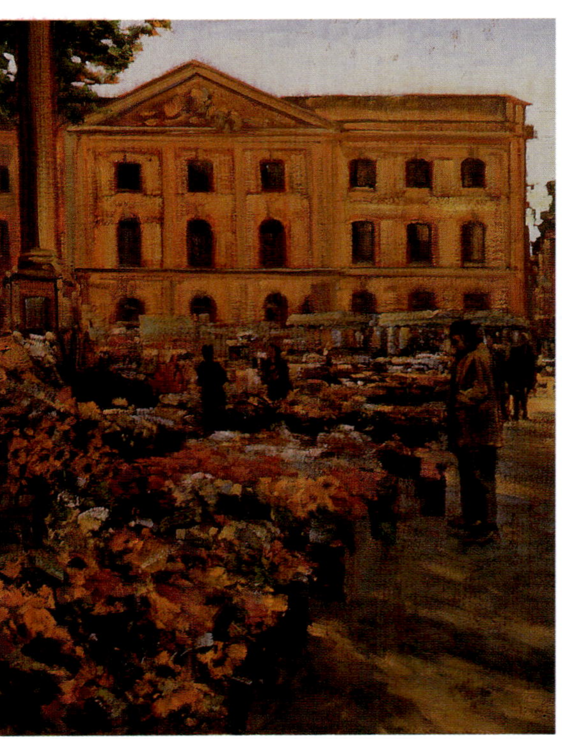

4 In this stage, I want to firmly establish the direction of the light source as I apply the mid-tones, which I create by adding more titanium white to the dark mixtures from step three. First I use a small acrylic flat brush to apply the tints of the flowers with loose and playful strokes. Then I begin lightening the areas in the middle ground, following the pathway of the morning light. I also define the tree on the left with a mix of sap green and cadmium yellow medium. And I fill in the sky, applying titanium white mixed with a small amount of phthalo blue in a gradation, using lesser amounts of blue as I work my way down toward the building.

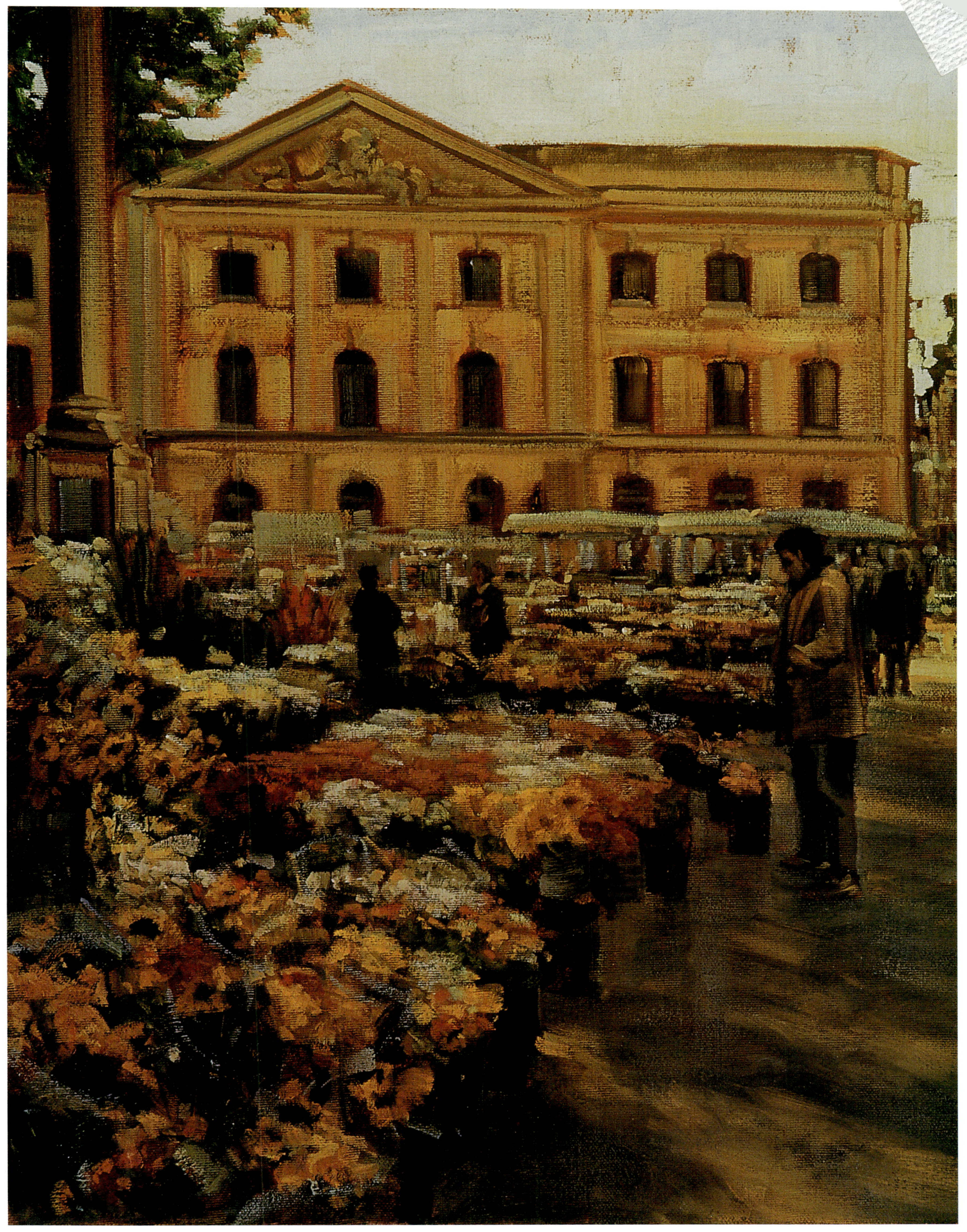

5 Still using the mid-tones from step four, I define the main figure's face and clothing with a small flat brush, applying the strokes carefully but with loose, easy movements. Next I begin painting the highlights. With a mix of titanium white, lemon yellow, and cadmium yellow medium, I add the highlights on the flowers, stroking on the color with a light touch so I don't disturb the darker colors underneath. To finish this scene, I stroke little highlights of pure titanium white on the market umbrellas and a few other objects; these pure highlights further emphasize the direction of the morning light while adding a sense of crispness to the scene.

Walter Foster Art Instruction Program

THREE EASY STEPS TO LEARNING ART

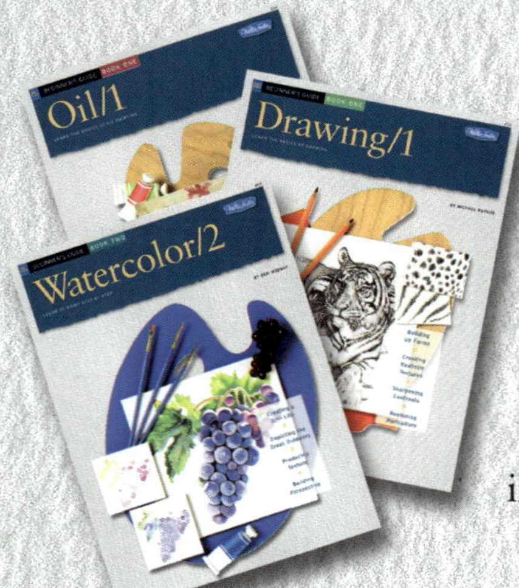

Beginner's Guides are specially written to encourage and motivate aspiring artists. This series introduces the various painting and drawing media—acrylic, oil, pastel, pencil, and watercolor—making it the perfect starting point for beginners. Book One introduces the medium, showing some of its diverse possibilities through beautiful rendered examples and simple explanations, and Book Two instructs with a set of engaging art lessons that follow an easy step-by-step approach.

How to Draw and Paint titles contain progressive visual demonstrations, expert advice, and simple written explanations that assist novice artists through the next stages of learning. In this series, professional artists tap into their experience to walk the reader through the artistic process step by step, from preparation work and preliminary sketches to special techniques and final details. Organized by medium, these books provide insight into an array of subjects.

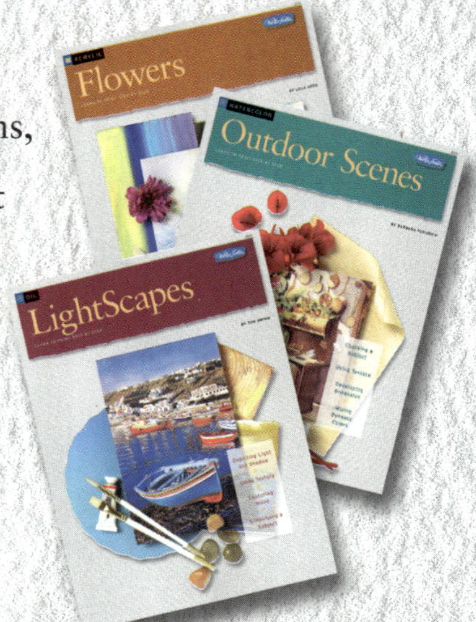

Artist's Library titles offer both beginning and advanced artists the opportunity to expand their creativity, conquer technical obstacles, and explore new media. Written and illustrated by professional artists, the books in this series are ideal for anyone aspiring to reach a new level of expertise. They'll serve as useful tools that artists of all skill levels can refer to again and again.

Walter Foster products are available at art and craft stores everywhere.
For a full list of Walter Foster's titles, visit our website at www.walterfoster.com
or send $5 for a catalog and a $5-off coupon.

WALTER FOSTER PUBLISHING, INC.
23062 La Cadena Drive
Laguna Hills, California 92653
Main Line 949/380-7510
Toll Free 800/426-0099

www.walterfoster.com